KT-074-984

Wimborne Minster

Jude James
December 1982

Wimborne Minster

The History of a Country Town

Jude James

THE DOVECOTE PRESS

To Michael and Jane Hanham

First published in 1982 by the Dovecote Press
Stanbridge, Wimborne, Dorset
ISBN 0 946259 00 9

© *Jude James 1982*

Designed by Humphrey Stone

Photoset in English Times
Printed and bound in Great Britain

All rights reserved

Contents

Origins and Early History   9

From Conquest to Stability   16

Church, Town and Property   20

The Medieval Parish   29

Upheaval and Crisis   37

The Years of Transition   53

An English Country Town   69

Appendix   88

Notes   91

Select Bibliography   94

Acknowledgements

The writing of a history such as this is only possible through the help of others. Sir Michael Hanham generously made available the family estate archives and told me much of the Hanham family background. Miss Margaret Holmes, the Dorset county archivist, Miss Hofman and other members of her staff were, as always, unfailingly helpful. Miss Mildred Holmes the former librarian of the Priest's House Museum and her successor, Mrs D. Nicolls, helped greatly with both archives and pictures. Miss H.M. Coles with her great knowledge of Wimborne filled many gaps in my knowledge. The honorary curator of the Priest's House Museum, Mrs Margaret Coe, gave every assistance and much help as a member of the 'Wimborne History Workshop.' The many members of that 'Workshop', organised by the Wimborne W.E.A. Branch, from 1976−82 have been immensely helpful in gathering material, analysing it and in debating its historical significance have contributed greatly towards this final distillation.

The facilities granted by the Dorset County Museum through the good offices of the curator, Mr Roger Peers, are warmly acknowledged. I am grateful, too, for access to the History Sources Room and the British Government Publications Library in the Library of the University of Southampton.

Amongst others who have helped me with information are Mr Bob Machin, Bristol University Resident Tutor in West Dorset, who supplied information on probate inventories deposited in the P.R.O. Mrs Norah Maisey for information on the Wimborne Minster Chained Library and on the church. The late Mr Charles Gibson of High Hall provided me with information and access regarding that estate. I am particularly grateful to Mrs Dawn Tucker of Modderfontein, S.A., for assiduously typing most of the Hanham Court Books and for her research into Wimborne's history. A number of townsfolk have provided me with information and anecdotes all of which have widened my appreciation of Wimborne's heritage.

I thank my wife for her patience and advice and, lastly and most particularly, my publisher, David Burnett, for labouring so hard with my rather unwieldy manuscript to make it suitable for the general reader.

Hordle
September 1982

JUDE JAMES

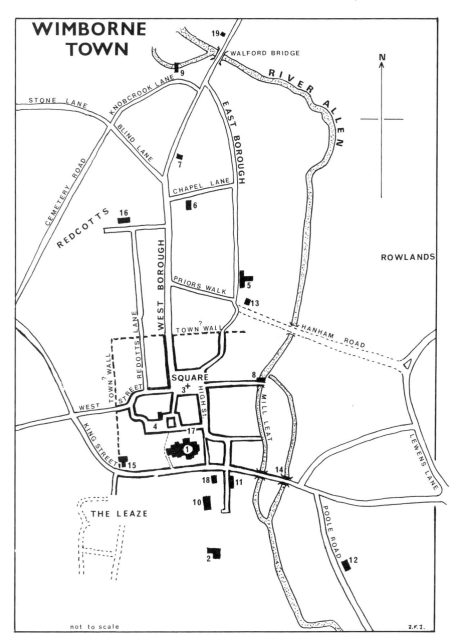

WIMBORNE TOWN

Wimborne Town

Heavy lines mark the main Deanery part of the town. The town walls are conjectural.

1. Wimborne Minster church (St. Cuthburga)
2. Dean's Court (The Deanery)
3. St. Peter's church (site of)
4. The Cornmarket
5. The Workhouse
6. The Congregational Church
7. Site of the first Baptist Chapel
8. Town Mill
9. Walford Mill
10. Queen Elizabeth Grammar School (site of)
11. Lady Gertrude Exeter's Almshouses (site of)
12. Police Station
13. Allendale House (1823), Castleman family
14. Eastbrook bridge
15. The National School
16. The County Primary School
17. Cook Row
18. The Methodist Church
19. Walford Turnpike toll-house (later The Case is Altered, now The Crown & Anchor)

ONE

Origins and Early History

It is inevitable that the mention of Wimborne Minster should conjure up the vision of a bustling Dorset market town dominated by the twin-towered minster church. But the town is only the urban hub of a large and prosperous rural parish in which the life of a town-dweller and countryman are intimately interwoven. In telling the story of Wimborne Minster it would not be right to separate these two elements. The town was, and is, the focal point for trade and communications − and by virtue of its size it inevitably dominates the life of the entire parish. And yet, without the agricultural wealth generated in the surrounding countryside, it would be difficult to imagine the development and growth of so vigorous a town.

The large parish, comprising nearly 12,000 acres by the 19th century, probably developed some time after the founding of the minster church and the establishment of the monastic community. Virtually nothing is known of Wimborne's history prior to the coming of the Saxons, and there is no clear evidence of a settlement in the area of the town during the Roman period. The nearest Roman settlement was at Badbury Rings (Vindogladia), near the site of the Iron Age hillfort. There was a major Roman base just south of the Stour at Lake Gates, and near Badbury Rings there was an important crossing of Roman roads to Hamworthy, Dorchester, Old Sarum and Bath.

Two of these roads do cross the Wimborne parish boundary, but the discovery of three cinerary urns in Wimborne Cemetery, 20 coins at Kingston Lacy and pottery sherds at Chilbridge Farm and Lodge Farm possibly indicate the importance of the roads rather than a settlement in Wimborne. Indeed, such a settlement seems even more improbable when balanced against the proximity of the Roman base at Lake Gates.

With the Saxons we are on safer ground. The area of the parish of Wimborne fell within the kingdom of the West Saxons, a kingdom established following the conquest of the region in a series of 5th and 6th century battles. The early evidence for Wimborne is so scarce and erratic that any interpretation of its origins remains largely conjectural. It is not even possible to firmly date the drawing up of the parish boundaries, but these are likely to have been confirmed by the time William the Conqueror had completed his great Domesday survey in 1086.

What is clear from the geography is that the site for urban Wimborne was chosen to lie between the Rivers Allen (formerly the Win) and Stour. This is further reinforced by what is known of the origins of other Saxon towns (Wilton lies between the Rivers Nadder and Wylye, Wareham between the Frome and Piddle). However, recent investigations[1] have suggested that the original Wimborne settlement may have been on the eastern side of the River Allen in the area known as Rowlands. It may well be the case that this

A view of East Street in the late 19th century.

9

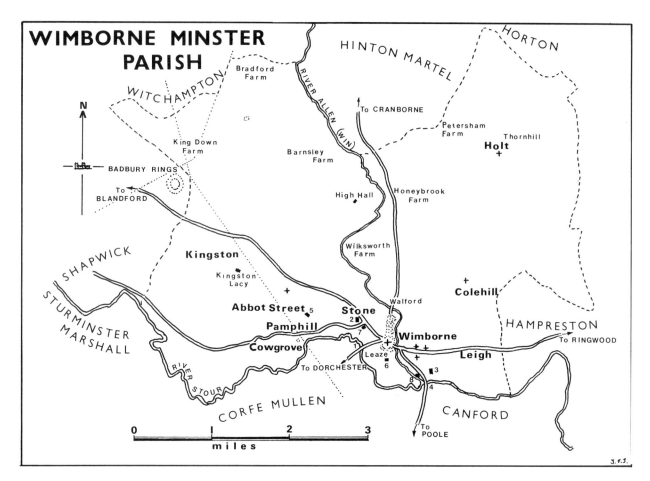

WIMBORNE MINSTER PARISH

Wimborne Minster Parish
Broken line indicates parish boundary prior to 1884-96. The dotted lines indicate the routes of the Roman roads and the dotted circles major Roman finds. The town area is shown by stippling. Only the principal roads and rivers are shown.

+   marks the site of present or former churches/chapels.
1. Julian Bridge
2. St. Margaret's Almshouses
3. Railway Station (1847)
4. Canford Bridge
5. Roger Gillingham's Almhouses and School (1698)
6. Dean's Court (formerly the Deanery)
7. The Victoria Hospital (1887)
8. Site of the paper mill

higher ground was selected by the first settlers to avoid the hazards of flooding, and that only after the building of the monastery between the rivers did they abandon their site. But we cannot be certain, and it is still not clear whether Wimborne grew as part of the pattern of English settlement or as a direct result of the establishment of the monastery in the early 8th century.

The first written mention of Wimborne occurs in the *Anglo-Saxon Chronicle* under the year 718. The entry states: 'In this year Ingeld, the brother of Ine, passed away, and their sisters were Cwenburh and Cuthburgh; and that Cuthburgh founded the monastic community at Wimborne.'[2] The words 'at Wimborne' might suggest that the foundation took place alongside an already existing community, but again it is impossible to be sure.

It is, however, clear that after the establishment of the monastery on land belonging to the royal house of Wessex the secular community flourished alongside the ecclesiastical − although we hear no more of it until 871 when the *Chronicle* concludes a description of Danish military successes in Wessex with the sentence: 'And afterwards, after Easter, kind Athelred died, and he reigned five years; and his body lies in the monastery of Wimborne.' Athelred was Alfred the Great's elder brother, and plainly, by this date, Wimborne was a place of sufficient importance to house the mortal remains of a king. The year 871 is also of interest in that it marks the first mention of the suffix 'minster' in connection with the town. The word

The Minster Church from across the Stour. An 18th century engraving also showing to the right of the church the Grammar School with its surrounding wall.

Boating in Poole Road after the Allen overflowed its banks during the winter of 1915.

11

The 15th century brass that commemorates the burial place of Athelred, king of the West Saxons, who died in 871 – dated incorrectly on the brass as 873.

means a parent church to several smaller churches, and by the 13th century the town was generally known as Wimborne Minster.

Thirty more years were to elapse before the *Chronicle* again mentions Wimborne. The entry is particularly revealing, for it states, after first describing the death of Alfred the Great, that:

> Then Ethelwold ... seized the (royal) manor at Wimborne ... Then the king (Edward) and his levies rode until he encamped at Badbury Rings, near Wimborne, and Ethelwold remained inside the manor with the men who had given him their allegiance; he had barricaded all the gates against them declaring that he meant to stay there alive or dead...

Ethelwold, in revolt against his cousin King Edward, had entered Wimborne to abduct, seemingly with her consent, a nun in the monastery. It was a venture in which he failed, for he later rode off in the night to join the Danish army in Northumbria. The tale may give spice to the entry, but it is most significant for describing Wimborne as having gates that can be closed against a military assault; and this strongly suggests that during the protracted period of Viking raids, Wimborne, as a royal centre, had been provided with defensive walls or embankments – perhaps similar to those that still encompass three sides of the neighbouring town of Wareham. A word of caution however. Although some have argued that Wimborne was a 'defended place' and even indicated the possible line of the defences[3], it was equally possible that the barricading of the gates of the manor (which is what the *Chronicle* states) indicate a defence round a residence rather than around a community. The Wessex towns provided with defensive walls were listed in a document entitled the *Burghal Hidage*[4], and Wimborne is not included.

It is, I think, important to include these details – if only to suggest the very significant problems that are encountered in attempting to describe Wimborne's origins and early development.

The evidence for the early religious life of the town is a little clearer. The religious community was specifically founded by Cuthburga on land granted to her by her brother, King Ine of Wessex. Ine had exceptional talents, and did much to give real substance to the role of the Christian church in his kingdom. It was he who divided the large and unwieldy diocese of Wessex into two parts by creating a cathedral at Sherborne in 705 and appointing Aldhelm as bishop for the western part of Wessex, an area that included the whole of Dorset. But the evidence for the foundation of Wimborne's monastery is not without contradictions, and it is impossible to give a precise date to its establishment. As we have seen, the *Chronicle* of 718 stated that 'Cuthburgh founded the monastic community at Wimborne...' But a letter by Bishop Aldhelm, referring to the freedom of the monasteries within his diocese to elect their own abbot or abbess, specifically mentions 'the nuns in the monastery by the river which is called Wimburnia presided over by the abbess Cuthburga.'[5] This letter is authentic, and it clearly proves that the ecclesiastical foundation at Wimborne took place between 705, when Aldhelm became bishop, and his death in 709.

The conversion of the pagan Saxons of Wessex had only occurred around the middle of the 7th century, but within the next hundred years Christianity had become widespread. Ine was a Christian monarch who had created a seminal law code of great significance for his kingdom. Just as

Christianity had shaped his thinking, so also had it affected his sister. Cuthburga had been given in marriage to the king of Northumbria, no doubt as part of a dynastic arrangement, but she was not attracted to married life and, with her husband's consent, she renounced her nuptial vow and entered a nunnery. Once her years as a novice were over, and no doubt as a result of her influence, she was able to found the monastery at Wimborne with the help of her sister, Cwenburh.

From the outset, the nuns of Wimborne would have required a priest or priests to conduct the sacraments, so there must have been some provision for their accommodation. Additionally, however, either Cuthburga or her brother founded a 'cloister for monks' within the monastery.[5] The resulting 'double' monastery was the largest in Wessex, with perhaps as many as 500 nuns. The male and female communities probably shared the same church for divine offices, but they lived separate lives, and even visiting bishops were forbidden to enter the women's quarters. Cuthburga died in 727, and little is known of her character. But without her, Wimborne's history might have been very different and, until the Reformation, a mass was celebrated in her memory on August 31st every year.

The achievements of the early church in Wimborne were considerable. The royal connection endured under Ine's successor and the training of nuns continued. One of the more famous figures to emerge was Lioba. She was sent by the abbess to Germany with thirty nuns in the steps of St Boniface to found a nunnery in Franconia. Her work was successful, and she helped extend Wimborne's influence into Europe; but St Lioba never

The north side of the Minster Church viewed shortly before the major alterations of the 1850s. The roof-line of the north transept against the tower is clearly seen: the later rebuilding restored the former roof pitch.

The Saxon stair-turret built in brown heathstone rubble in the north transept – the oldest part of the Minster Church standing above ground.

returned to her community in Wimborne, dying in a monastery near Mainz in September 757.

There can be little doubt that so important a monastery as Wimborne's, built on royal land, would have had a beneficial effect on the secular community that lived in its shadow. Skilled craftsmen would have helped meet its needs, and they in turn gave impetus to the growth of the town. Food, wool and leather would have come from the surrounding countryside, forging links that still endure between the urban and rural communities.

A curious and unexplained entry in the *Chronicle* dated, 962 refers to King Sigferth who 'killed himself' and whose body was interred at Wimborne. It has been suggested that Sigferth was an imprisoned Danish monarch who had died in some form of accident, but the truth is unlikely to be known.[6] What it does seem to indicate is that Wimborne was still, despite Viking raids, an important monastic town.

There is little physical evidence for the early monastic buildings. The discovery of a fragment of coarse tessellated flooring beneath the floor of the minster nave during restorations in 1857[7] only whets the appetite for further clues. This piece of mosiac pavement, between two and three feet square, may represent a part of the floor of the monastery. Sections of 11th century walling, dating from the late Saxon period, do survive in the present minster church, particularly in the north transept.[8]

Like so much of Britain, the monastery suffered its own 'dark age' throughout the years of the Viking raids into Wessex. Its history went unrecorded, a fact that may be explained by the probable destruction of the monastery by the Danes in 998.[9] It is one of the eccentricities of Wimborne's history that whilst many records of the monastery in the Middle Ages survive, we have to wait for the itinerant topographer John Leland to report in the mid-16th century that 'King Edward' converted the monastery, or its remnants, into a house or college for secular canons with a dean at its head. The Edward may well be Edward the Confessor (1042 – 1066)[10], but the changes that befell the religious community must await the chapter on medieval Wimborne.

One of the greatest and most permanent debts we owe to our Saxon (or Old English) forefathers lies in the contribution they made to English place-names. The vast majority of these names date from the Saxon settlement in Wessex of the 5th century onwards. These early names often provide valuable clues (sometimes the only clues) to local topography and the ways in which the land was being developed and used.

Wimborne itself is derived simply from a river name Win-burnan. The River Allen was known to the Saxons as the Win(n), meaning 'meadow'. The 'burnan' part is the origin of what we call a 'borne', meaning a stream or brook. Hence Wimborne is the 'meadow-stream'. Other local names are more descriptive, for example the rising ground to the north-east provides a number of names ending in '-hill', such as Cole-hill, Thorn-hill, Furze-hill and Linen-hill. Thornhill and Furzehill are self-explanatory, but Linenhill may derive from the 'hill where flax is grown' (as linen is made from flax). The 'Cole-' element in Colehill is probably derived from 'charcoal', thus suggesting the hill on which charcoal was produced.

The lower or valley areas also have their own distinctive names. Cowgrove is straightforward, the 'grove' being a woodland clearing. Similarly Leigh is derived from the common Saxon word 'leah', again

Cowgrove, showing the farm and a timber-framed cottage.

meaning a glade or clearing: hence, also, Barns-ley. Holt means a wood and in its earliest forms is called 'Winburneholt', or the 'wood near Wimborne'. The fact that both the rivers Stour and Allen possessed shallow, wadeable crossing-places is revealed by the 'ford' in such names as Walford, Barford, Bradford and Canford. Only Pamphill defies easy interpretation, but the word 'pamp' does occur as a surname in many medieval deeds relating to the town.[11]

TWO

From Conquest to Stability

At Christmas in 1085 William the Conqueror (1027 – 1087) met with his councillors at Gloucester to hold 'important deliberations and exhaustive discussion' about the country he had conquered nineteen years earlier. It was there he decided to carry out a survey of the whole kingdom that would record details of land-holding, taxes due on land, the agricultural uses and value of the land, the livestock it carried, the status of those who occupied it, enumeration of water mills, salterns and much other information. The result was the magisterial *Domesday Book* of 1086. An earlier version, known as the *Exon* (or *Exeter*) *Domes-day* and covering sections of the south-western counties, was completed shortly before the compilation of the Exchequer version. Wimborne appears in both.

The feudal system introduced by William I into England meant that all power and ownership of land was the prerogative of the crown. Every person, whether baron, cleric, or minor nobleman, held his land from the king. Those who did so were known as tenants-in-chief, and each of them, in turn had the right to grant part of his land to others. Payment in return for land-holding was almost wholly by means of service; either in the form of providing military service, the performance of specific tasks, or in labour (such as ploughing or harvesting). It was a society structured like a pyramid with the crown as its pinnacle and the lowest serf at its base. Despite gradual modifications to the system, it was, in outline, the form of government under which Wimburnians lived and worked throughout the Middle Ages.

The descriptions culled from *Domesday* present a lively portrait of feudal society, and the hierarchy it supported. Serfs occupied the bottom rung on the social ladder, for they lacked even the freedom to marry without their lord's permission. Above them came the cottars and bordars, both of whom were small-holders who cultivated their own land but worked for others for their livelihood. Next came the villeins, a widespread and important class who both farmed their own land and worked for their lord in exchange for their holdings. The villeins were the first to finally gain their liberty, and many were quite prosperous.

Above these groups of unfree peasants were the minor free-men. In the context of Wimborne they are described as 'thanes' and a few, such as Godwin the huntsman, Dodo and Ailrun, held moderately-sized agricultural holdings directly from the crown. Above them ranked the lords who came with William from Normandy, men such as Robert Fitz Gerold who held the estate of Leigh. The highest rank of all comprised the barons and noblemen who held their estates directly from the king as tenants-in-chief.

What *Domesday* gives us is the first really reliable evidence and detailed information on Wimborne. It also provides a glimpse of the town in the late

Saxon period, for it was a feature of the Survey to compare England immediately before the Conquest with all that had taken place since William's victory at Hastings.

Unfortunately, the evidence provided by the Domesday Surveys is not entirely straightforward. The Dorset section begins with a list of towns which includes Dorchester, Bridport, Shaftesbury, and Wareham – but not Wimborne. Should we be right in thinking, therefore, that Wimborne was not an urban centre? The position is not clear. The lands that comprise Wimborne are contained in several distinct entries, one of which (for Hinton Martell) mentions burgesses in Wimborne. It has been concluded that Wimborne 'seems to have been a substantial agricultural settlement with an urban element.'[1]

The first entry in the *Exeter Domesday* relating to Wimborne states that William I, and his predecessor, Edward the Confessor, hold one manor 'which is called Wimborna and Escapewihc (Shapwick) and Chirche (Crichel) and Obpe Winborna (Up Wimborne).' It is not possible to separate the four parts of this large and sprawling manor and decide which tells us about Wimborne itself. Being royal land none of it paid any tax, but it was certainly an important agricultural holding containing sufficient arable land to employ no fewer than 45 plough teams. Of these, 5 worked directly for the king on his demesne (land worked directly for the landowner by the unfree tenantry). The villeins had 22 plough-teams for their own use. The king had 15 serfs on his demesne, whilst 63 villeins occupied the remainder of the manor. Other members of the community were 68 bordars

An 1857 engraving of Wimborne showing the surrounding agricultural parish. Only later in the 19th century did the suburbs begin to spill out over the fields.

17

Walford Mill. The present buildings date from about 1800, and the mill was once one of two important corn mills in the town.

and 7 cottars. This, perhaps, indicated that the total population of the manor was somewhere between 600 and 700.

Livestock records list 250 sheep, 44 goats, 30 pigs and 3 pack-horses. No direct mention is made of oxen but their numbers can be estimated from the number of plough-teams; perhaps a total of 250 would not be unreasonable. The manor also contained an extensive tract of woodland, a large area of pasture and 150 acres of meadow. The amount of grain grown was obviously considerable, for there were 8 water-mills in the manor.

Although not burdened by taxation, the manor was expected to produce enough to pay for one night's residence for the king and his entourage whenever he was on a circuit of his kingdom. Such a levy helped reduce the burden of costs on the particular residence in which the monarch and his company stayed.

The entry in the Exchequer *Domesday* virtually repeats that contained in the fuller Exeter account. Both remark that as the manor was royal property there was no means of stating its total acreage. The entries do little to help us understand the precise position of Wimborne, but as it was the first to be named it was probably the largest element in the manor.

A further entry describes half a hide[2] (about 60 acres) of land called Winburne — land owned by the king but held by his wife, Queen Maud. The estate was small, with only two plough-teams. In addition to the arable there was a small area or woodland and 14 acres of meadow, and the entire estate was exempt from the one night's tax for the maintenance of the royal court when travelling on circuit. Both versions state that the holding was worth £4, the same value as it had been in the time of King Edward. The Exeter version also mentions 2 beasts (oxen), 127 sheep, 30 goats and 10 pigs.

Several other entries in Domesday refer to Wimborne within other manorial units. Probably the most significant is the entry for 'Hinetone' (Hinton Martell). After describing the royal manor of Hinton the entry goes on to state that the Bishop of Lisieux in Normandy (about 30 miles east of Caen) and a priest hold certain land there including 11 houses in Wimborne and that, in its turn, the church at Wimborne owns 150 acres plus some land at Hinton Martell, and that there are 6 bordars and 8 burgesses. The mention of burgesses is significant, for presumably they occupied the 11 houses. A burgess held for a money rent and free of all services a plot of land in a town. It was a form of land-holding known as burgage tenure, and its existence is taken as one definition of a borough. On this tenuous evidence it may be said that Wimborne was a borough in 1086.

The other entries with references to Wimborne are Horton, which states that the Benedictine monastery there had a chapel at Wimborne, and Canford Magna, where the land held by Edward of Salisbury as tenant-in-chief included one house at Wimborne with 3 bordars and a league of marshland. These latter entries strongly suggest that there was an urban community in which houses and a church, in addition to the monastery, were held as part of rural manors lying beyond the boundaries of the parish.[3]

Wimborne, as a rural estate, granted special status to those who occupied the land. In the surrounding rural areas the landholders were all minor noblemen who held their farmland directly from the crown. Of these we can cite Wilksworth (Wedechesworde) as an example. Here the agricultural estate lying just to the north of the town was divided into two. On one there was a single plough-team worked for the owner, Dodo, by 2 serfs; whilst elsewhere on the estate 2 villeins and 2 bordars had between them half a plough-team. There was also 14 acres of meadow and a stretch of woodland, and the unit was valued at 10s.

Another hundred acre estate was situated between Wilksworth and Wimborne. *Domesday* calls it 'Walteford', meaning the present Walford. This was held, like the Wilksworth estates, directly from the king by Godwin the huntsman. His single plough-team estate was valued at 15s., which suggests that it was somewhat more productive than those at Wilksworth.

Leigh lies to the east of the town on the rich, flat alluvial soils beside the Stour. Here a French nobleman, Robert Fitz Gerold, had replaced the two Saxon thanes who had formerly held the estate — valued in their time at 13s. Fitz Gerold's appearance is of political interest, for it shows the extent to which native Saxons had been replaced by Normans as land-holders in the area. He probably lived at Povington in the Purbecks[4], and the land was worked by 3 villeins and a single plough-team. It boasted both meadow and woodland, and its value had increased to 20s. by 1086.

Another important estate lay in the north of the parish at Petersham Farm, where there was perhaps a windmill. This, like Wilksworth, was divided into two units, and both had a single plough-team to work the arable. Once again the Saxons had been dispossessed, for the Saxon owners of both units had been replaced by Frenchmen.

There are two other estates recorded in *Domesday* which are believed to lie within the parish, but neither can be identified with any certainty. One was Odeham (Odenham), which was held by the Bishop of London, and the other was Selavestune, a valuable estate of nearly 450 acres and worth 60s.[5]

To summarize Wimborne at the date of *Domesday*, we can perhaps imagine a small and flourishing township with the monastic church at its centre, but also having a smaller church or chapel belonging to the Benedictine monastery at Horton. Surrounding the town lay farmland, with its mixture of arable, woodland and meadow. Sturdy timber-framed mills lined the rivers, for the main crops were undoubtedly wheat and barley. The meadows provided the vital hay crop for feeding the livestock during winter. Cattle and sheep grazed the rougher pasture land, and the woods provided fuel and building timber as well as forage for pigs (especially acorns and beech-mast). There is no direct evidence as to how the land was worked, but it seems certain that the surrounding arable was divided into strips and farmed collectively by the peasantry. The overall impression given by *Domesday* is of a prospering parish; of a wooded landscape broken by fields and rivers, and the thatched roofs of a town that was dependent on farming for its livelihood.

THREE

Church, Town and Property

Throughout the Middle Ages the influence of the church embraced all aspects of English life. It was as much concerned with the secular life of the people as it was with their spiritual welfare. Nothing was ignored that could add to its prestige, and, as its power and wealth increased, so too did charity and education come increasingly within its orbit. All these elements of ecclesiastical life play their part in Wimborne's history.

After the destruction of the old monastic community at the end of the 10th century, it was replaced by a college of secular canons. Initially this comprised a dean who in theory had overall responsibility for the affairs of the church and its community. Beneath him were four prebendaries (each of whom was a canon and whose stipend was drawn from the endowment of land and estates). There was also a sacrist responsible for the furniture, fitting and supply of the church. In addition to the original complement of clergy four chaplains were gradually appointed to serve the chapels in and around Wimborne: St Peter in the Square, St Catherine at Leigh (nearly opposite the present Catholic church), St James at Holt and St Stephen at Kingston Lacy. Additional clergy were eventually endowed to care for the chantries as they were founded.

The college was a 'royal free chapel', meaning a chapel directly under the monarch's patronage and free of the control of the diocesan bishop. (Wimborne's diocesan history has been varied: from 705 to 1079 it was part of the diocese of Sherborne, from 1079 to 1542 part of Salisbury, and until 1836, when it was returned to Salisbury, it was included within the diocese of Bristol). The freedom granted to Wimborne's church allowed it to control its own liturgical arrangements and maintain its own ecclesiastical courts, dealing with matters as diverse as morals and probates. The royal patronage led to the title usually being given as a 'Royal Peculiar.'[1]

No details of the endowment of the church survive, but originally it probably consisted of the great tithes.[2] Certainly by the 13th century the church at Wimborne was well-endowed with lands and rents. We do know that in 1291 Pope Nicholas levied a £71 tax on the church, based on the value of its endowments, and proof of its growing prosperity.[3] By 1318 the dean was able to include Shapwick, Little Crichel, Hampreston, Stanbridge and Kingston Lacy in a list of the 'pensions and portions' that gave the church its wealth.[4]

The independence of the royal free chapel was central to its survival, and the royal concern for maintaining its independence was proved beyond doubt when in 1238 the Bishop of Salisbury and Archdeacon of Wells tried to appoint a William de Badeston as a priest to Shapwick church. The church belonged to the Wimborne deanery and Henry III, on principle, objected to this overriding of his authority and forbade the appointment.

He also refused them the right of appeal to the Pope — proof of royal stubbornness when his ecclesiastical authority was in question. We have further examples of royal intransigence from Edward I, who in 1307 forbade the collection of dues from Wimborne Minster and successfully prevented all attempts by the cardinal's office to coerce the dean and chapter into making the payment. The keen regard for the independence of the Royal Peculiar by successive monarchs could hardly be better demonstrated.

During the first half of the 13th century, probably in the 1220s and 1230s, considerable extensions were made to the minster church. The chancel was largely rebuilt and extended as a Lady Chapel, and both the north and south transepts were lengthened.[5] The basic Romanesque core survived, but the rebuilding remains a superb example of the Early English Gothic. Much of the rebuilding was in limestone, but the newly favoured Purbeck marble was effectively used to provide dark and contrasting shafting round the lancet windows at the east end of the Lady Chapel (now the Chancel). Unfortunately, no records have so far been uncovered that tell the story of the rebuilding. But the work must have boosted the town's commercial importance, for it provided employment for large numbers of masons, carpenters, carters and labourers.

The deans throughout this period were Martin de Patteshull and Ralph Brito, both influential men who took advantage of their status to add to their prestige. de Patteshull, appointed dean in 1224, was also a justice of

The Square: the dogs stand on the site of the former town church of St Peter's. In the centre of the picture East Borough winds away from the Square, hence its alternative name 'Crooked Borough'. Richard's Family Hotel (The Crown) has since been demolished, as have the neighbouring 17th century cottages.

The interior of the Minster Church looking towards the great west window. Four round-headed arches, built in the 12th century, spring from massive pillars to support the central tower.

the King's Bench, a prebend in St Paul's Cathedral and Archdeacon of Norfolk. In 1228 he was appointed Dean of St Paul's whilst continuing to hold office in Wimborne, a town he may never have visited. Ralph Brito combined his spiritual power with more worldly posts. As well as Dean of Wimborne, he was also Constable of Colchester Castle and Warden of the Essex ports. That both men had no shortage of ambition and energy is obvious, and it may have been one of them who instituted the rebuilding of the minster.[6]

The most famous of Wimborne's deans was Reginald Pole, appointed in 1518 when still only eighteen years old. As a cardinal, he was twice elected Pope, but on both occasions he refused to take office.

The post of Dean of Wimborne was often a stepping-stone to higher office, as well as being a reward for services rendered to the crown. Even the canons took advantage of their influence to reap other harvests. In 1300, Robert de Vanna received permission from Pope Boniface VIII to hold livings in the dioceses of Lincoln and Carlisle and yet remain a prebendary canon in Winborne.[7] Thirty-five years later, in a less typical case, Pope Benedict XII granted dispensation to John Rotecod of Wimborne Minster, 'the illegitimate son of a married woman,' and allowed him to be ordained a priest and hold a benefice.[8]

The examples of absenteism by successive deans brought little credit to the medieval minster church, but they do provide a valuable insight into the extent of its property. In 1338 three clergymen were charged to look into the defects of 'the hall, chamber, chapel, kitchen, grange, stable, oxhouse, piggery, walls, fences and mill' which had occurred during the incumbency of the last dean, Richard de Clare. They later reported that the defects could be put right for £28.3s.[9]

Even worse neglect occurred during Henry de Bukyngham's period of office. After his death in 1367 it was discovered that 'no less than £400' would have to be spent on repairs to the deanery buildings. The buildings stood on the south side of the minster, adding a hint of the farmyard to the more cloistered world of the canons.

Also attached to the minster were its chantries − small chapels in which chaplains celebrated mass on behalf of those who had founded them. The earliest was the Great Chantry, founded in 1354 by Thomas de Brembre four years after being appointed dean, and often known subsequently by its founder's name.[10] The right of patronage to the living at Shapwick was transferred from the dean's holdings to the maintenance of four chantry priests, and after Brembre's death the custodian of the chantry and the priests were granted a licence to acquire land and rent at Walford, Chilbridge, Colehill and an unidentified place called 'Duppleshegh'. That same year a local landlord was granted the right to give the income from crown lands to the chantry. It was a generous gift, for it included 16 acres of meadow, 5 acres of pasture, 2 acres of wood, and pasture for 16 oxen, 12 cows, 40 pigs and 400 sheep. The total value of the estate was over £71, providing an annual income of £4 to the custodian and chaplains of the chantry. Sustained by such endowments, they were left in peace to pray for de Brembre's soul.

Throughout these years the town was slowly expanding on its site around the minster church. A traveller entering the town had a choice of approaches, and once within its boundaries the road would have been filled with pilgrims come to see the relics in the minster, craftsmen selling their wares from open doorways, peasants and yeomen returning to their homes

The Minster Church, looking east to the triple lancet windows above the altar. These, decorated with Purbeck marble shafts, were added in the 13th century. Simple scalloped capitals support the ornate arches of the transition from Norman to Gothic architecture.

Each chantry had its own seal to authorize documents. The one illustrated belonged to Brembre's Chantry and shows the Blessed Virgin Mary above the arms of the founder.

23

West Borough in about 1860. Prior's Walk turns off at the end of the railings on the left. The large round-headed entrance on the right still survives.

from the open fields, and carts and pack-horses laden with the canvas wrapped bales of raw wool that were adding to Wimborne's wealth. The principal roads ran north through Walford, east through Leigh, south through Canford and west towards Corfe Mullen. A north-western road sloped uphill towards Pamphill and Blandford. The condition of medieval roads varied: most were rutted in summer and a quagmire in winter. In Wimborne's case, the perils of flooding added to the hazards facing the traveller. Wimborne Minster and Kingston Lacy were on the royal itineraries of both Henry III and his son Edward I, and the main routes into the town were well maintained. We know that Edward visited Wimborne five times between 1275 and 1306.[11] All these visits took place during the winter, a fact that perhaps explains the three large casks of wine sent from Southampton to Kingston Lacy in November 1252 to await the king's arrival.[12]

It was during this period that the town spread south from the minster church into the fields now known as The Leaze. Partial excavations in the early 1960s have helped provide a glimpse of this medieval community and its single-roomed dwellings clustered either side of the street. Settlement in The Leaze appears to have begun in about 1200, finally extending to perhaps forty houses. No coins were found by the excavators, but the cooking pots, bowls and jugs (all typical pottery of the period) that were unearthed tell us a little about the life of the community. Those who lived there may well have tenanted small allotments from their landlord, probably the dean,[13] and the bellowing of their livestock would have added to the din in the growing town.

It has been suggested that the town was deliberately extended into The Leaze by the dean, a practice initiated by the bishops of Winchester as a method of creating new boroughs (as at Downton, Wilts).[14] The suggestion

24

becomes even more interesting if we consider the possibility that both East and West Boroughs were a creation of the lords of Kingston Lacy and intended to compete with the town.[15] The markets held in these boroughs were rivals to those of the dean, making friction inevitable. In 1277, Jordan Lockey, a stall-holder, was setting-up his standing 'to the annoyance of the free market of the dean.'[16] Lockey argued that his stalls had been there since Martin de Patteshull was dean; and we can reasonably conclude that they were situated in a market uncontrolled by the dean, either in East or West Borough.

Wimborne's first market had been established prior to 1218, for it was then that the dean obtained permission to hold it on Mondays instead of Sundays. The market provided the church with an income, and the tolls levied on stall-holders passed into its coffers. In 1224 it was ruled that the market should no longer be held in the churchyard, but somewhere outside the walls on land belonging to the dean. The ruling may have taken the market into the Cornmarket, in which case the Cornmarket itself owes its evolution to the change of site.[17]

The disputes grew more numerous. John de Lacy claimed that the dean's market was harmful to his own, even taking his case to court. His grandson, John de Lacy, submitted a claim during the reign of Edward I to hold a fair on St Cuthburga's Day (September 3rd) and a market on both Sundays and Mondays. Such disputes were not easily resolved, and they continued to trouble the town throughout the Middle Ages.

The Cornmarket in 1981 after its conversion into a 'plaza'. The George Inn once stood in the Cornmarket, but the White Hart is the only inn to have survived.

Yet the arguments are evidence of expansion, of merchants and craftsmen struggling to break the church's grip on the commercial life of the town. Most were self-made, born in a tenement or rural cottage, and their determination to share in the town's prosperity is understandable. As well as being proof of Wimborne's growth, the creation of The Leaze by the dean, the market's move from the churchyard, and the establishment of East and West Boroughs by the lords of Kingston Lacy give a hint of the jostling for power that went on as Wimborne developed.

Further evidence of the town's growth is provided by the taxes levied on its inhabitants in 1327, 1332 and 1334. The tax was based on an assessment of the value of moveable property and was levied as a proportion of the value, but it did not cover the clergy, and is therefore described as a Lay Subsidy. The portrait these taxes provide of the medieval town is often surprising. For instance, not only was Kingston Lacy wealthier than Wimborne, it also was more densely populated (see Appendix, Table I).

We know nothing of the buildings in the early medieval town. Most were probably of wattle and daub, as yet without window-glass or chimney and with only rushes on the floor. Those of the wealthier townsfolk may have been partly timber-framed, or even of stone. But we do know something about the manor house at Kingston Lacy, to the west of the town. The name Kingston means 'king's farm', and is first mentioned in about 1170. Although owned by the crown, successive monarchs occasionally granted

Lodge Farmhouse, probably the oldest domestic building in the parish. The farmhouse, which is in Pamphill, is built in local heathstone with 13th century gothic windows carved in limestone on the first floor. It is just possible that the house was built in the 17th century using older stone, perhaps from the medieval manor house at Kingston Lacy.

the estate to others. In the 12th and early 13th centuries it was held by the Earls of Leicester and various members of their families. In 1229 it was granted to John de Lacy and given the name that still survives. It later reverted to the crown, either to be held directly by the monarch or again be granted to favoured nobility, such as the Earls of Lancaster. To the king and aristocracy it was merely one of many estates — at best a favourite hunting-lodge, or perhaps only a source of revenue. But although those who held it had little direct influence on the life of Wimborne Minster, the manorial courts that operated on their behalf did have an affect on the community. All those who held land on the estate had to appear in court before their landlord's steward to fix the details of their tenure. Similarly, the estates of the dean and college maintained their own manorial courts in the town.

The site of the original great hall at Kingston Lacy has vanished without trace. In a nearby cottage there are a pair of limestone columns supporting a beam over the fireplace, and these may have come from the medieval hall.[18] On the rising ground to the north of Court Cottage at Cowgrove there is an earthwork. This may mark the original site of the manor house,[19] or even an open-air meeting place for the manor or local tithings. By the 1490s the uncertainty ends, at least over the materials with which the manor house was built. The Wimborne Churchwardens' Accounts refer to 'stone bought at Kingston Lacy' for 22s., and the 7s. paid to 'Simon the labourer' and others for 'cast downe stone at Kyngston,' evidence suggesting that the house was being demolished. Further proof of demolition is provided by John Leland when writing about Kingston in 1540, for he notes that 'Ther hath beene a fair manor place caullid Kingston-haul and this is now in a manner clearly defacid.'[20]

Despite Kingston Lacy's importance, it was no more immune to disaster than Wimborne itself, and in 1348 all expansion in the town was abruptly halted by the arrival of the Black Death. The plague entered England through Melcombe Regis (now part of Weymouth), and Dorset was the first county to be struck by the epidemic. Somewhere between a third and half the total population of England died during the Black Death, and Wimborne must have suffered considerably when it reached the town. No accurate population figures for the town are known, but the Lay Subsidy Rolls do allow a rough estimate of 1,430 in the parish on the eve of the Black Death (See Appendix, Table II). The plague periodically reappeared throughout the rest of the Middle Ages, claiming Thomas de Brembre in 1361 only seven years after founding his chantry.[21] The Black Death marks a watershed in English history, and it is perhaps apt that one possible result was the desertion of The Leaze.[22]

FOUR

The Medieval Parish

Farming in the parish has always been governed by the differences in its soils — soils which vary from the rich alluvial loams of the river valleys to the sands and gravels in the east and north. As early as 1086 much of the area was devoted to pasture for livestock. Sheep formed the backbone of the local economy. A flock of 250 grazed the royal estates, and by the mid-14th century there were 400 on de Corfton's land at Kingston and Colehill. Flocks like these provided wool, meat, milk, bone and horn: parchment was made from their skins. They were folded on the fallow, manuring and enriching the ground for the corn crop that followed. As well as giving employment to a shepherd and local butchers, others depended on them for a living: the merchants and middle-men who sold the raw wool, the clothiers in the town, the woodmen who coppiced the hazel woods and wove it into the wattle hurdles used during lambing. Cloth and wool dominated England's medieval export trade, and the proximity of Wimborne to the southern ports must have shaped its economy and added to its wealth. The name Shapwick means 'sheep farm,' and by 1327 its taxpayers included a William Bercario, which is the Latin for shepherd.[1] Five years later the surname 'Shephurd' is amongst those listed in Leigh.[2] A good shepherd enjoyed a status to match his importance. Many were permitted to run a few sheep of their own with their employer's flock, and in 1374-5 the shepherds at Kingston Lacy were receiving an annual wage of 5s.[3] in addition to their clothing, food and rent.

Indirect evidence of the value of sheep comes from the tithes levied on lambs and wool, and there are many incidental references to them in the Wimborne Church-wardens' Accounts — as in 1403 when 3s. 4d. was received for four ewes and 10s. for 'this year's new wool.'[4] Later accounts mention the payment of 10d. rent for 'a piece of pasture large enough to feed 5 rams and one hog until shearing time' (probably from April to July).[5]

If sheep were a key element in the farming calendar, the ox was the principal beast of draught — as is shown by the number of plough-teams recorded in *Domesday*. The arable fields surrounding the town were probably worked on a two-field strip culture, one remaining fallow whilst corn was grown on the other. With time, the system was modified into the more effective three-field rotation (winter corn, spring corn, and fallow), and the patchwork of long open fields in the parish must have provided the town with much of its flour.

By the mid-14th century the open fields were already doomed, the depopulation following the Black Death and the creation of family-worked holdings encouraging the beginnings of enclosure. By 1786[6] the only open fields in the parish lay in Kingston Lacy, and they survived in a rather emasculated form. In the Middle Ages, the open fields were controlled by

Early 20th century peace contrasts starkly with late 20th century bustle. Two views of the Square.

29

The Market House in the Cornmarket, built in 1758. Usually, these market houses had an open lower floor to allow traders to set up their stalls.

the manorial courts, and it was the courts that decided on crop rotation and the precise times of sowing and harvesting. In theory, but not always in practice, the tenantry exercised certain common rights which no landlord could ignore. These included the cutting of turves for fuel, and pannage — the right to let pigs forage through the woods in the autumn.[7]

As well as marking the introduction of enclosure, the 14th and 15th centuries saw the gradual ending of serfdom. The first known commutation from unfree tenure in Kingston Lacy occured in 1408-09 when out of a total of 78 villeins 17 secured their release.[8] However, certain services still had to be performed, and as late as 1485 the tenants on the estate were carrying out their winter duties 'according to custom'[9]; probably threshing, cutting timber, and some ploughing. Another obligation that still had to be met was attendance at the manorial courts. Fines had to be paid when first tenanting land, and all such arrangements were entered into the court rolls. Such tenancies were known as 'copyholds' (i.e. held by copy of court roll), and in

30

Wimborne parish most land was held in this manner until well into the 19th century.

The status of the peasantry was no different to that of the townsfolk. Their lives and preoccupations were too similar to foster a distinction between town and country. By law, all journeymen and apprentices were obliged to help gather in the harvest; meadows, piggeries and cowstalls could still be found in the town centre. The larger proportion of Wimborne's population were poor, illiterate craftsmen who shared roof and board with their apprentices. Many of these men were employed in the cloth trade, for the turning of raw wool into cloth called not for one craft but many — washing, carding, spinning, weaving, fulling and dyeing. Wool was processed in the town, and some cloth was undoubtedly manufactured. Evidence of the cloth trade still survives, for the Southampton port register mentions Wimborne carters carrying woad and madder for dyeing and alum for fulling. In 1443, for example, 'John Bodyn from Wymbournemynstre (came) with vii balett waid and i bale alym' for the merchant John Govayr.[10] There was a fulling mill for pounding cloth into felt on the Kingston Lacy estate, and the Churchwardens' Accounts refer to the income from both coarse and new wool.[11]

Tanning was another important local industry, and there was at least one 'tanner's shop' in the town.[12] Tanning is proved by names such as John the Tanner and Henry the Skinner, whilst the two men named 'Boteler' were probably makers of leather bottles.[13]

Unlike many towns in the south, Wimborne's economy was never entirely based on sheep. Its position as a route centre and the presence of the minster attracted a wide range of skills and gave variety to its commerce. Wheelwrights, blacksmiths and carters built and operated the waggons that rumbled through the narrow streets. The minster church and newer settlers required tilers, masons, glaziers, plumbers and carpenters. The list is interesting, for it means that by the beginning of the 15th century tiles and stone had begun to appear amongst the houses in the town. The use of tiles, fixed with nails to wooden laths, is mentioned in 1413 — a year that includes the purchase of sand and lime by the churchwardens for making mortar. A later purchase refers to 200 bricks, suggesting the existence of local kilns to provide the town with building materials. Chimneys are also mentioned, but such luxuries were rare, and most houses in the town were still open-hearthed and timber-framed, their wattle and daub walls decorated with pargetting.

This blend of building styles must have added to the town's attractions, giving it an air of confidence and self-sufficiency. Itinerant tinkers attended its markets (as in 1496 when one was employed to mend pans at a cost of 4d.). There was a 'Pybaker's house' and both a meat and fish shambles. The taverns offered a refuge from the bustle. The cook-shops that lined Cook's Row provided townsfolk and travellers alike with a selection of ready-cooked foods. Other goods mentioned frequently in the records include platters and treen dishes, linen, silk, rope and oil. The town had its own chandler, who as well as supplying candles and tapers to the town must have been kept busy meeting the demands of the minster church.

The church seems to have occasionally defeated even the most adaptable of craftsmen in the town. Holy oil came from Salisbury, as did a set of new candlesticks in 1511. In 1495 it was a man from 'Ryngwode' who was summoned to do work on the church bells.

Despite such lack of loyalty, the church's involvement in the life of the town was considerable. The dean's court controlled the tenure of shops and stalls, and appointed the portreeve responsible for collecting the market dues and rents, recorded by the churchwardens as 'portreeves silver.' The portreeve also made certain that the tradesmen did not defraud their customers, and in 1524 he was issued with weights and measures to assist him. They were kept in the Yelde Hall, the town guild hall in which the dean's court also met. The site of the Yelde Hall has long since vanished, but it was probably situated in the Cornmarket and the meat shambles may have occupied the ground floor. It was in the guild hall that the tradesmen and craftsmen gathered to regulate their affairs, and by the late 15th century they were paying an annual rent of 5s. for its use.[14]

As well as the Sunday and Monday markets maintained by the dean and lord of Kingston Lacy, there were at least two major annual fairs – both of which added to the revenues of the minster. The medieval fair was a celebration of the town's spirit – and of its purchasing power. Prices were always unpredictable, for they fluctuated according to the quality of the harvest and prevailing market conditions. In 1374 barley was 6d. a bushel. A pig fetched 3s. 6d. and a ewe 1s. 3d. Oats then sold for 5d. a bushel, but by 1446 the price had fallen to 3d.[15]

Wimborne's fairs would have attracted traders from throughout the south, as well as the minstrels, mummers and travelling cheapjacks who crowded the inns. St Cuthburga's Fair was held on September 3rd, and there were two additional fairs at Pamphill, one in October and the other in late December on St Thomas the Martyr's feast day. In 1268, Henry III granted Holt the right to hold its own fair, doubtless because it was growing fast and a fair in the village would have served the parishes to the north of Wimborne. A century later John, Duke of Lancaster (the then holder of Kingston Lacy) was granted the right to hold a further fair near the chapel of St James.[16]

The pleasures of Wimborne's fairs hint at a portrait of the town that is perhaps not entirely accurate. The desertion of The Leaze sketches a more sobering picture, for the Black Death was only the most spectacular of a whole succession of epidemics that raged throughout the middle ages. Famine and disease were commonplace. The streets were open sewers piled with refuse and manure. Many villagers lived at subsistence level, and their fellow parishioners in the town often fared no better. The 14th and 15th centuries were renowned for a succession of bad harvests, and in some years sheep murrain reduced the flocks to only the breeding ewes. If the wealthy were better equipped to face potential disaster, few were immune to its effects, and the lack of fresh vegetables throughout the winter made scurvy a familiar sight.

Leprosy was also common, and wealthy benefactors, supported by the church, often established hospitals for the care of lepers. Wimborne was no exception, and one such hospital stood on the Kingston Lacy estate at the point where the ancient road to Cowgrove turned west towards the river. Little is known of its early origins. It may have been founded by William Fitz Parnell, himself a leper, whose elder brother Robert, Earl of Leicester, held the manor from 1190 until his death in 1204.[17] Another less likely tradition argues that the charity was established by John of Gaunt (1341 – 99), Edward III's fourth son, but foundation undoubtedly took place at a much earlier date.[18]

An 18th century sketch of St Margaret's Chapel.

St Margaret's Almshouses in 1905, the chapel is visible on the right.

The hospital was dedicated to St Margaret and St Anthony, and in 1245 Pope Innocent IV granted a 51 years and 260 days indulgence to all its benefactors. The relevant Papal Bull is mentioned in a 16th century deed, which also states that the hospital was not endowed but maintained entirely by alms. There are few records of its early occupants, but a Kingston Lacy court roll dated 1398 mentions the admission of a William Sharpe to the hospital by the steward of the manor. After seven years Sharpe was maliciously expelled by a John Tripet, and he had to petition the court to be re-instated.[19]

A chantry was established at the hospital early in its history by John Redcoddes, whose name (as Redcotts) is given to land and a lane nearby. By 1438 it owned several tenements in the town, providing an income for the maintenance of a chantry priest.[20] The little early 13th century chapel still survives, though within the last few years some of its medieval features, including wall-paintings, have been obliterated by restoration. Its wealth must have once been considerable, for amongst its possessions were two basins of silver and gilt, and three silver chalices weighing a total of 55 ounces.[21]

Like caring for the sick, the maintenance of roads and bridges was often regarded as a Christian obligation. In 1341 Richard Bryan left by his will 3s. for the repair of White Mill Bridge near Sturminster Marshall, a bridge in Blandford and one in Wimborne: in Wimborne's case it was probably the bridge over the Stour on the road to Poole that benefited from his bequest.

Repairs to both bridges and roads were a costly but necessary expense, for their traffic was heavy. Carters moved to and fro between the town and Southampton with materials for the cloth and wool trades; others brought such goods as 'gryndyngstone', wines, fish-pickle and fruit. Purchases of Caen stone by the churchwardens had to be loaded onto flat-waggons on the quay at Poole and laboriously hauled to Wimborne.

Complaints about the state of the roads were many, but that by the villagers in Hampreston of 1440 may well have had an ulterior motive. Because the village lacked its own burial-ground, the dead had to be carried the two miles to Wimborne along a road that was 'muddy and deep in wet weather and commonly flooded by the river Stoure, so that four or five days together pedestrians cannot pass there, whereby corpses are kept so long above the ground that men abhor to bury them or to pass with them to the ... place of burial.[22] There was probably some substance to their argument, for the residents of Holt made a similar protest in 1493, but it is likely that they overstated it in order to strengthen the case for the provision of their own graveyard — a graveyard that was in fact granted by Henry VI.

Alterations to the minster church continued throughout the Middle Ages. Alterations to the east end in about 1350 allowed the construction of a crypt beneath the chancel. Just over a century later, in 1459, the construction of the massive west tower saw the last major addition to the building. The work took several years (the churchwardens were still buying stone in 1464, e.g. 31 loads at a cost of £4. 10s.), and it must have provided employment for a large contingent of craftsmen, including the travelling masons whose lean-to 'lodges' erected as temporary shelter have survived in the language of freemasonry. Sadly, the early offer in the form of a grant to take stone from Sir John Benton's Hampreston estate was not taken up, and the 95 feet high tower was built in greensand stone carted from a now unknown quarry called 'Woodmansheet', perhaps somewhere in the Shaftesbury area where there are a number of greensand quarries. Had stone from Hampreston been used, it would have been much more in keeping with the rest of the fabric.[23]

Perhaps the most remarkable medieval addition to the minster was its astronomical clock. It has been convincingly argued[24] that the clock was constructed in 1375, and in 1409 the churchwardens hired a carpenter to make it a case and provide it with a lock and key. Although not unique, it must have astonished the townsfolk, for then, as now, it was widely regarded as a triumph of clock-making. Perhaps only those who had to pay its running costs were suspicious of so ingenious and mechanical a device. If built in 1375, it cost over £5 in maintenance and repairs in its first century of life — the approximate equivalent of 21 years wages to a shepherd or ploughman.[25]

As well as the minster, there was a second town church, St Peter's, which stood on the site of the present square: in 1414 its churchyard was enclosed by a fence or wall at a cost of 8s. 6d.[26] Little is known of St Catherine's chapel at Leigh, but it was certainly in use throughout the Middle Ages and some repairs to it were carried out in 1439-40. St Stephen's at Kingston Lacy was originally founded in the 13th century as a place of worship for the lords of the manor and their servants, but it was soon being used by all those who lived on the estate. It too was repaired in 1439-40, but it seems to have been neglected for in 1573 it was recorded as 'being beyond repair'.[27]

The other main church in the area was St James's chapel at Holt. St

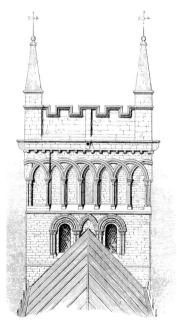

The west face of the central tower showing the ornate arcade of round-headed arches. The 12th century tower has recently been much restored.

34

Wimborne Minster Church lit by floodlights.

James's may have been built at about the same time as St Stephen's, for there is a reference to two chaplains in a grant dated 1284 to Henry de Lacey, and it was certainly in existence by 1368 when a charter was granted for a fair to be held in the village. For a time its chaplains were endowed by the Augustinian Priory of Christchurch, and it only finally gained its independence when Henry VIII permitted the appointment of a chaplain 'in perpetuity.' As with Hampreston, the villagers found an ally in the state of the roads, 'being separated from the parish church of Wimborne by obstacles and the road between is long and remote and in the winter is so noxious and muddy that the inhabitants of the hamlet are unable to get to the Church without grave and tedious labour.'[28] One wonders, however, what the 'obstacles' were that prevented attendance at Wimborne Minster but allowed the villagers to drive their livestock to its markets?

One name, above all others, remains associated with medieval Wimborne: that of Lady Margaret Beaufort (1443 – 1509), Countess of Richmond and Derby, and mother of Henry VII.

Her impact on the town was immense, and her virtues are best summed up by the oration given at her funeral by her friend Bishop John Fisher (later to be executed by her grandson, Henry VIII):

All England for her death had cause for weeping. The poor creatures that were wont to receive her alms, to who she was always piteous and merciful; ... to all devout and virtuous persons to whom she was a loving sister; all good religious men and women whom she was often wont to visit and comfort; all good priests and clerks to whom she was a true defender...[29]

An etching of the Beaufort tomb, erected by Margaret Beaufort in memory of her parents, John Beaufort, Duke of Somerset, and Margaret Beauchamp.

Lady Margaret's involvement in the life of the town began when she paid for an elaborate tomb in the minster in memory of her father, John Beaufort, 1st Duke of Somerset, and her mother, Margaret Beauchamp. The tomb shows husband and wife lying side by side, hands clasped, united in death after a marriage that had ended with Beaufort's probable suicide.[30]

Bishop Fisher encouraged Lady Margaret to take an interest in the endowment of schools, as a result of which she founded colleges at both Oxford and Cambridge. Her endowment to Wimborne was on a much smaller scale, but to the townsfolk it had a far greater significance. After creating a chantry in the south chapel of the minster alongside the Beaufort tomb, she went on to link it with the establishment of a grammar school. Her death in 1509 prevented her from seeing her plan reach fruition, and it fell to her executors to purchase the land and appoint a chaplain. The first chaplain was Sir (a courtesy title, for he was not a knight) Richard Hodgekynnes. He lived apart from the dean and canons of the college, residing permanently in the house where he taught grammar 'to all who came for instruction, according to the custom of the schools of Eton and Winchester.' As far as is known the school continued to function until dissolved with the chantry in 1547.

Following Lady Margaret Beaufort's death, an anniversary mass was celebrated every July 9th, on which occasion £1 was distributed in her memory in the following manner:

To the sacrist of the college	1s. 4d.
To every chaplain 'devoutly singing'	8d.
To every secondary and parish clerk	4d.
For the bell-ringers	8d.
For 5 wax candles and bell ropes	1s. 4d.

The residue was distributed to the poor of the parish at the rate of either 1d. or 2d. according to their needs.

Lady Margaret had taken holy vows five years prior to her death (she never entered a nunnery), and her devotion to her faith inspired her to leave two copes of blue and gold cloth and a suit of vestments to the minster in her will.[31] Such devotion as hers was soon to seem a relic of a more generous age. Within forty years of her death, her grandson Henry VIII had caused the greatest spiritual upheaval ever known in English history, and with it brought the Middle Ages to an end.

FIVE

Upheaval and Crisis
1529-1700

In 1529 Henry VIII's Reformation Parliament began a seven year sitting. When it rose the death knell of the Middle Ages had been sounded. The king, angered by the Pope's refusal to allow him to divorce Catherine of Aragon and marry his pregnant mistress, Anne Boleyn, had set into motion a chain of events that completely changed English society. The Reformation had begun, and it was to be carried through with all the injustice and dogmatism that normally attends a social revolution. It marks a turning point in Wimborne's history, not only because Henry VIII's decision to break with Rome and declare himself head of the Church of England reshaped the spiritual map of the town, but because its effects filtered down through every level of society, leaving no one untouched. Dissent, poverty and upheaval were to be the milestones that marked Wimborne's struggle to adapt to all that had happened.

Initially, worship at the minster church and in the chapels of the parish remained undisturbed by the Reformation. But the peace could not last, and in 1547 the wheels of dissolution were set in motion with the appointment of commissioners to examine the chantries and report on their wealth. Twelve years earlier a similar report had been compiled, providing a financial portrait of the wealth of the chantries and college on the eve of dissolution. The college was then valued at over £95, but by 1547 its value had fallen to just over £51[1] – a clear indication of the uncertainty bred by the Reformation. The minster had been badly neglected. The building was 'in great ruin and decay and our tower is foundered and like to fall.'

The Chantry Commissioners wasted no time in acting on their report. Both Brembre's and Lady Margaret's Chantries were dissolved and the College of Canons was abolished. Censers, relics (which are supposed to have included hairs from Our Lord's beard and part of His robe) – anything that smacked of Romanism – were removed from the minster. Reformist zeal had no time to stop and count the cost. The ten altars were demolished, the ornamental plate was sold, and by the end of the century the religious paintings on the walls had been covered with whitewash.

The Chantry of the Hospital of St Margaret and St Anthony was also dissolved, and responsibility for running the charity was placed with two parishioners, elected annually, who were to be styled the guardians or wardens of St Margaret's Hospital or Almshouse.[2] Prior to the dissolution, the chantry's income came from the rents on two pieces of land on the Kingston Lacy estate. The land was now returned to the Duchy of Lancaster, owners of the estate, and the chantry chaplain, Simon Benyson, was pensioned off at £5 a year.

The 1563 seal of the Corporation of the Free Grammar School. The minster is shown prior to the collapse of the spire in 1600. Note the rows of boys and the schoolmaster holding a birch as a symbol of his authority.

To assist them carry out their survey and draw up an inventory, the commissioners employed a local lawyer, 'Master Phyllypes'. In addition to the £1 he was paid, Phyllypes was entertained to dinner at 'Dewey's' at the expense of the churchwardens — a dinner that required the purchase of five quarts of wine from 'Mr Lovell's for ye comyssernes.'[3]

Reaction within the town to the dissolution of the College and chantries must have been varied. The seeds of dissent had perhaps been sown as early as 1539 when 'certain riotous persons led by Sir Giles Strangways' went on the rampage during the fair armed 'with swords, bills and other weapons.' After wounding a farmer, they turned on a priest, who only escaped by 'slipping from his gown' and escaping into the churchyard. But on one point the townsfolk were united — their anger at the closure of the school and Lady Margaret's Chantry. They soon complained, saying that the school was 'very requisite and necessary' in a 'great market town.' They also reminded the commissioners that with no other grammar school within twelve miles of the town they had little opportunity for educating their children. The commissioners were sympathetic, offering to support the town in its attempt to found a new grammar school.

The Churchwardens' Accounts catalogue the interim arrangements that kept the old school alive between the dissolution and the founding of its replacement. A schoolmaster was employed and appeals were made in London to the king's council to try and force a decision.[4] Finally the parishioners enlisted the help of the redoubtable James Blount, Lord Lieutenant of Dorset and owner of Canford. Blount's persuasiveness accelerated the final victory, and in 1563 Elizabeth I granted Wimborne a charter for the establishment of a corporation to run both the town and a new grammar school. As the parish was crown property (the combination of the Kingston Lacy estate and the possessions of the deanery), she was able to support the new school with valuable endowments. All the land held by the chantries had also reverted to the crown, and her charter lists tithes at Barnsley, Kingston Lacy and all the lands that had formerly belonged to the four prebendaries. Interestingly, these tithes were still in the possession of the Corporation of the Grammar School when the tithe apportionment was made in 1846. In return for these grants the Corporation paid the crown £40 a year, in two instalments.

The Charter of 1563 laid down that the Corporation should comprise 12 governors, chosen from amongst the 'most discreet and substantial inhabitants' of the parish.[5] It was to have its own seal and the power to sue or be sued. Out of its revenue it was to pay for a schoolmaster, three priests and three clerks. The years saw certain amendments to these original provisions, and in 1639 by letters patent Charles I released the Corporation from royal control 'in consideration of £1,000 paid into the Exchequer'[6] and created the Grammar School free to all his subjects for the education of their sons. It was also given a new name, the Grammar School of the foundation of Queen Elizabeth in Wimborne Minster. As well as a schoolmaster and an under-teacher able to teach the 'science of grammar', it was stated that 'there should be in the church of Wimborne Minster three priests and three clerks to celebrate divine office and discharge the cure of souls of the parishioners there, and four choristers, two singers, and one organist to assist in the celebration of divine service.'

One of the Chantry Commissioners employed in 1547 had been Poole's M.P., John Hannam.[7] A Hannam was a natural choice as a governor of the

Queen Elizabeth Grammar School. The upper illustration shows the 18th century school, the lower illustration the mock-Elizabethan school built to replace it between 1849 and 1851. The building is shortly to be converted into town flats.

*John Hannam, M.P. for Poole
and purchaser of the Wimborne
deanery estates in about 1550 – a
detail from a posthumous portrait
hanging in Dean's Court.*

Corporation, and the appointment of his son Richard marks the beginning of an involvement by the Hannam family in the life of the town that has spanned four centuries. Sir Michael Hanham, the present baronet, lives in Dean's Court, and it was John Hannam himself who acquired the deanery estates and made the dean's house his home. Little is known of John Hannam, but it seems probable that he was typical of the ambitious and talented Tudor civil-servant who used his influence to serve his own ends. His son, Richard, entered the Middle Temple, establishing a link with the legal profession that finally bore fruit when no fewer than six members of the family were elected to the Long Parliament of 1640.[8]

The Bankes was the other distinguished family to make its mark on post-Reformation Wimborne. Sir John Bankes initiated the involvement with Dorset when he purchased Corfe Castle and its estates in 1634.[9] His wife, Lady Mary, is remembered for her courageous defence of the Castle against Parliament during the Civil War. Their son, Ralph, later to be knighted, purchased the Kingston Lacy estate in 1647, finally building the house that stands there today.

The minster was not the only church to be affected by the Reformation. The town church of St Peter soon suffered from neglect and by 1588 it was reported to be decayed. The church stood in an acre of ground, which was finally sold to Thomas Hannam.[10] The year after his purchase he vested the property in the Corporation to enable it to build a town hall. This was built with a shop beneath and a tenement at the west end that was leased out by the Corporation. The town must have had little pride in its new town hall. It was badly built and then neglected. Eventually it fell, leaving an area of waste ground in the centre of the town that was left untouched until the 19th century, when it was cleared and turned into what is now the Square.

The Reformation had international as well as domestic repercussions. Threats gave way to the possibility of invasion, causing Henry VIII to react by ordering the construction of defensive castles along the south coast (as at Sandsfoot, Portland and Brownsea) and the establishment of a local militia, composed of ablebodied men and armed with whatever weapons were available. The first Wimborne muster took place in 1539, and the parish was divided into various tithings: Abbot Street, Barnsley, Cowgrove, Leigh, Stone, Thornhill (covering Holt), Wimborne Borough and Wimborne town.

Although there was no shortage of men willing to serve in the militia, their weapons would have been no match for an invasion force. The most common was the bill-hook; many were armed with the long bow and a sheaf or half-sheaf of arrows; some owned a light body armour comprising a breast and back plate, and a few had a protective helmet. Perhaps prudently, Richard Russell of Barnsley alloted his armour to his servant, whilst Robert Townley (as his name suggests he lived in the town) could muster harness for his horse, a pole-axe, a bill and a spear. Those equipped with battle-axes, swords and daggers were perhaps the most military, but some of the townsfolk carried no arms at all and there is no mention of any form of firearms.[11]

The early Tudor muster rolls show that a small number of Frenchmen were living in the town, adding to its increasingly cosmopolitan atmosphere. As early as 1525 the name 'Gyllam Frenschman' is recorded as an 'alien.' There were eight in 1539, probably merchants or journeymen who had

Kingston Lacy, the north front of the original 17th century house built for Sir Ralph Bankes from designs by Sir Roger Pratt.

settled in Wimborne to carry on the cloth trade. By the time the next subsidy was levied six years later two of them had become naturalized – perhaps in response to the increasing threat of war between France and England.

Apart from the rich, most of the Elizabethan townsfolk in Wimborne lived in four-roomed timber-framed houses.[12] Their lay-out varied, but they traditionally consisted of a large hall or hall-chamber, a smaller downstair room and two bedrooms. In many cases, these upper rooms were no more than a semi-attic with dormer windows that looked out over the fields that still ringed the town. Craftsmen and tradesmen often added a lean-to extension in which they could practise their skills. Unfortunately, no buildings of the period survive in the town. The rural parish, however, can still boast a few survivals from the latter part of the 16th and early 17th centuries, though all have been considerably modified.

The Hearth Tax returns (See Appendix, Table III) of the 1660s show that out of a total of 402 houses 265 had either one or two fireplaces, and that 52 had five or more. Dean's Court (still at this time the medieval house) had no fewer than twenty-four hearths, suggesting a rambling manor house with at least thirty rooms. Kingston Lacy had yet to be completed, and the next largest house in the parish was Holt Lodge, the home of William Pitney.[13] Despite the timberframing and the continued use of wattle and daub, the infilling was starting to be of brick. Even in the countryside wattle and daub is now rare, but some has survived within the interior panels of a timber-framed thatched house at Holt called Crooked Withies.[14]

41

A timber-framed thatched cottage at Hillbutts, built in 1697. Cottages such as these were characteristic of many 17th century rural dwellings in the parish.

The hall was the principal room of the Elizabethan house, and usually the best furnished. In 1570 the hall of Thomas Baker's cottage at Holt had a table board, 2 old chairs and 2 forms (long seats without a back).[15] There was also an old cupboard in which were kept four plates and the other domestic utensils, including perhaps the three 'lyttyl' brass candlesticks listed in the probate inventory after his death. The four plates were probably reserved for special occasions, whilst for everyday use they had nine wooden dishes and a bowl. For cooking, his wife used a small frying pan and a little brass pan which stood beside the fire on a brass skillet. The hearth was the centre of cottage life. All the cooking was done on an open fire. The main fuels were turves, furze and logs, but some of the larger houses and town houses burnt coal carted in from Poole. In their hearth the Bakers had two hanging pot-hooks and a 'tostynge' iron or fork.

In their upstairs bedroom there was a coffer in which they kept their clothes. As well as the bedstead itself, they also owned two coverlets, one old sheet, one flock bolster and two feather pillows.

When John Delacourt died in the town in 1564 he left amongst his possessions the following items:[16] three flock beds worth 10s. each and another valued at only 2s., perhaps a child's. There were four coverlets to go on the beds and four pairs of sheets. In the hearth he kept several brass pots and ten platters, as well as a dripping pan worth 1s. to catch the fat from spit-roasted poultry and joints. He had two tables and a settle. There is no mention of knives, but the inventory lists a dozen spoons and two dozen trenchers. Delacourt was by no means wealthy, for his goods were valued at £6. 6s.

More substantial is the inventory of John Ase (or Ace), one of the chaplains of Brembre's Chantry.[17] It is dated 1568, and is indicative of the wealth of an educated but minor cleric. His goods were valued at over £43, and his wardrobe alone included 2 gowns, 4 jackets, 2 doublets, 2 pairs of hose, 3 night caps and 3 square caps. Ase was more prosperous than the average tradesman or small farmer (his eight spoons were of silver). But what really sets him apart from his contemporaries, and proves his intellect, is the ownership of a library. Books were still scarce and costly, and the ownership of 20 books in Latin and 21 in English would have alone made him wealthy.

In his will Ase left 6s. 8d. to the minster church, and a further 6s. 8d. towards repairs of the chancel. An additional £1 was left to the 'poor folk whose most nede ys.' Gifts of money for the repair of the minster were frequent in wills, as were clauses asking that money or goods be distributed amongst the poor. When a farmer, Thomas Frampton, died in 1583 he gave 10s. to the poor, 10s. to the minster and willed that his body be buried in the churchyard.[18] Even after the Reformation the lives of the townsfolk continued to be nominally controlled by the church. But its influence was on the wane. The charters granted to the Corporation of the Grammar School by Elizabeth I, James I and Charles I confirmed the Corporation's right to regulate the affairs of the community. Through its power to appoint priests to the minster (although with the sanction of the Bishops of Bristol) it was also able to control the appointment of the 'Official' of the Court of the Royal Peculiar. In reality, all the power and influence enjoyed by the dean and chapter during the Middle Ages had now passed to the Corporation. It was the Corporation who ordered the apprehension of vagabonds and the rounding up of stray animals, who fixed the hours for bells to be rung to open and close the market, who ordered the streets to be cleaned and supervised the collection of refuse. Dedicated to the principles of self-help, of no rights without duties, it encouraged civic pride and allowed Wimborne to develop its own identity and character.

The principal Official of the Peculiar Court was the judge, usually chosen from amongst the three ministers in the parish: later a layman was occasionally appointed. In court he was assisted by a legal advisor known as the Register. The court's strongest penalty was excommunication, but others included penances and fines, and the money levied in fines was probably distributed to the poor.[19].

The cases dealt with by the Peculiar Court ranged from charges of immorality to the proving of wills. Morals seem to have absorbed much of its time, usually in the form of accusations of sexual misbehaviour, as when in 1638 Jane Besant accused Anne Frampton of being a 'base filthy whore, a base filthy strumpet.'[20] Few courtesies were wasted on the niceties of the English language, and the charges of accusation and counter-accusation that were levelled evoke a less prudish and more rumbustious age. For instance, in 1579 William Jubber accused three women from Kingston of adultery, but his evidence was somewhat confounded when he in turn was accused of being seen in bed with a widow in someone else's house.[21]

Even the minster organist was not immune to such temptations. He was accused of immorality after being seen in Redcotts Field where, a witness said later, 'he had seen the new organ player (Robert Durman) ... play upon a new pair of organs in the said field with one Elizabeth May carnally', but when spotted 'he did take to his heels.'[22]

There is little doubt that many women succumbed to such advances on the promise of marriage. When accompanied by a sworn statement, the sexual act was regarded as a legitimate form of marriage by those involved. This was the case with Robert Yates and Alice Smith in 1591. Robert swore: 'Heare, Alice, I doe give thee my faithe and my trothe to marrye with thee, and doe take thee to my wieffe, and I will never marrye with anie other but

One of Wimborne's few remaining examples of timber-framing. A mid-17th century house near the Methodist Church.

43

thee whilst I live.' To which Alice replied: 'And I doe take you to my husband and doe give you my faithe and my trothe.' Whereupon the couple shook hands to seal the bargain.[23]

Accusations of immoral living crop up constantly in the records of the Peculiar Court, suggesting that prostitution was common in the town. In 1600 a woman called 'Whitelegge' was summoned for living in ' a lewd manner' and giving birth to bastard children. The case against her seems all too probable, for the name 'Whitelegge' evokes a reputation for enticement by lifting her dress to display her legs.[24] Another case mentioned by the records is that of a married woman who in 1613 was offered a pair of shoes by a Simon Parker 'to have the use of her body.'[25]

There were also a number of cases of men and women living together without having married. In 1640 John Purchas was brought before the court for living with Grace Spruce, and the following illustrates the punishment it prescribed:

He is enjoyned upon some Sunday betwist this and the next Courte to repaire to the Church of Wimborne Minster at the time of the reading of the second lesson at morning prayer ... and there apparelled in a white sheate with a white rod in his hand, stand upon the peninential stoole appointed for that purpose, confesse and say after the minister before the whole congregation as followethe, – 'Good people: I acknowledge and confess that for suspicion of incontinent life with one Grace Spruce of this parish, I was orderly called, and injoyned my purgation according to order of law and fayling the same I am now, therefore, worthily punished and taken as a man convicted of the crime. And I am heartily sorry that by my loose life and behaviour I have given cause of this offence and scandall, ad I doe desire God to forgive me...[26]

Some, it seems, were not moved by the fear of eternal damnation. When, in 1602, John Barnes of Holt was accused of living unlawfully with another man's wife, he told the court that he would continue to do so 'do what thou canst.' But not all the accusations were taken seriously, for in some instances an attack on morals masked an attempt to mar a reputation or denigrate an enemy – a strategy that was also used against Catholics who refused to conform to the rites of the Church of England.

For Wimborne's Catholics, the years following the Reformation brought hardship and persecution. Those who clung to the 'old religion' became known as recusants. A small enclave survived in the town, and in 1598 the following were listed as papists: Roger Loope and wife, Christopher Siler and wife, Comson Gilles, Robert Habgood, John Miller and wife, John Cornishe and wife, Edward Due, Henry Young and wife, Thomas Morris, Thomas Jay and wife, Joan Pinson and Margaret Trime.[27] Margaret Trime (or Trem) was amongst the most devout. Her behaviour was eventually reported to the Earl of Salisbury by Thomas Elliot on the grounds that the Trems were 'the worst recusants in Dorsetshire' and that Margaret had spoken 'wild words against the King at Wimborne. The report also stated that 'Mass is said in their house by a seminary priest and his ornaments are there: cope, chalice, pyx, holy water, with all other relics fit for Popery. Margaret has turned (i.e. converted) many people of late ... 40 persons come to that house to mass and Margaret keeps all the saints and relics in her house fit for them.'[28]

Thomas Elliot's report was made shortly after the abortive Gunpowder Plot of 1605, and his hatred for all things Catholic was well demonstrated by a letter to the king in which he described recusants as 'devilish, arrogant,

Two early 20th century views of East Brook Bridge.

44

perverse and damned traitors,' and recommended that they be 'quick lapped up alive in lead, with their arms spread abroad, and set upon the highest pinnacle in every city and port town in England, and there let them starve to death.' Faced by such bigotry, which was common, Margaret Trime's devotion seems all the more remarkable.

In opposition to Wimborne's Catholics, there was a second minority in the town that welcomed the break with Rome but did not regard it as having gone far enough. They were known as Dissenters, or Nonconformists, and their early history in Wimborne remains shrouded in obscurity. But Nonconformity undoubtedly had its followers, for in 1595 Alexander Fowler was excommunicated for 'blasphemously using the name of God': three years later both he and his wife refused to take communion. Fowler was moderately well-to-do, but the commercial isolation that went with excommunication little mattered if there was a body of sympathizers willing to ignore the ruling of the court. Fowler was again arraigned for non-attendance in 1597 and in 1604 he again refused to take communion.[29] Such persistence in resisting the law cannot be explained by mere wilfulness. Their faith supported such men and helped dissent to flourish.

Some of the clergy in the town also appeared to have shared Fowler's beliefs. Thomas Norman was appointed to the minster in 1597, and in 1610 it was reported that 'our preacher master Norman dothe not read divine service nor minister the sacraments of the lordes supper nor baptisme according to the Canon, nor wear such ornaments as is spesified in the booke of Canons.'[30] A year later the accusations were repeated, and a group of parishioners petitioned that he should be admonished by the Royal Peculiar. He remained unrepentant, and as late as 1616 he was still preaching despite having officially been 'silenced by the order of the Court of my Lord's grace of Canterburie.'

Men like Norman became more common as dissent spread. When Thomas Rowe, formerly rector of Lytchett Matravers, moved to Little Canford in 1666 he set up a meeting house in his home. He occasionally preached in Wimborne, and in 1672 he became the first minister to the newly-built meeting house in the town — a post he held until his death eight years later.[31]

The religious fervour of the period did little to encourage the expansion of the town. It also bred many eccentricities, ranging from accusations of witchcraft to sightings of the devil. Perhaps the strangest such case concerned a Mary Brewer who, whilst listening to a sermon in the minster, thought she saw the devil standing beside the priest in the pulpit. Later she returned to the pulpit, defecating where she believed she had seen the devil. Unfortunately for her, young Elizabeth Sandell happened to be in the minster at the same time and was suspicious of Brewer's behaviour. She approached the pulpit, finding in it 'excrement newly done.' Brewer then attempted to hide what she had done, first denying its existence and then saying that she was not responsible. The aged sexton was faced with the unpleasant task of cleaning the pulpit. For some reason the affair was not raised in the Peculiar Court until March 1602, nearly two years later.[32] It was an odd case, but not isolated, for similar acts of defilement have been recorded in connection with highly emotive religious states. Mary Brewer was not punished, perhaps gaining from the court the sympathy and understanding she needed.

Despite their difference, Dissenters and Catholics were united in their unwillingness to attend services in the minster conducted according to Anglican rites, and the most persistent offenders were excommunicated. They also objected to paying tithes on their produce to support a church which neither faction accepted. Those who refused were brought before the Peculiar Court, as in 1600 when eight people were arraigned from Cowgrove, three from Abbot Street, four from Leigh and six from Stone – including Thomas Elliot, author of the report about the Trime family. In 1621 William Eyers was actually excommunicated for his repeated failure to pay his tithes.

Not all cases of non-attendance at the minster were motivated by religious convictions. George Long regarded matins as a suitable moment to play bowls with his servant. Jane Clarke, no doubt with an eye to potential customers, kept open her shop for the selling of food and drink. A brickmaker named Deck found 'a common ale house' more congenial than the minster. When Richard Alim was discovered sitting in Cook Row by the church sidesmen he refused to accompany them to the minster and called them 'knaves and baggage fellows.' John Jay played the game of fives on Sundays as well as throughout the week, 'to the hurt and grief of the ministers.'[33] Fives were usually played in the churchyard, against the north wall of the minster, often causing damage: occasionally fives' players cut steps in the buttresses to gain access to the roof and retrieve lost balls (an example of this can be seen at Bradford Abbas).

So lengthy a catalogue of failure to attend the minster suggests that the church's authority was diminishing. But not all the day-to-day work of the Royal Peculiar was spent policing the religious beliefs of the townsfolk. The proving of wills took up much of its time, for it was the court's responsibility to make certain that the wishes expressed in wills were carried out by their executors. The wills themselves offer a glimpse into the domestic lives of the families concerned – and of their differences. Robert Cornish gave half his money to the poor living on the west side of Walford Bridge, but to his brother, who owed him £19 and 'had taken away a kettle from him which was like to break his heart,' he left nothing.[34] When Margaret Goldesney of Barnsley made her will in 1622 it was initially in favour of her son, William. But a later change of heart led her to make a second will, cutting him out because 'he has used her ill, cursing and abusing her.'[35]

Despite the shock waves caused by the Reformation, trade and commerce continued to dominate Wimborne life in the early 17th century. The town boasted butchers, tailors, carpenters, tanners, curriers, cutlers, collarmakers and braziers. There was a woman who made coverlets and a fish shop kept by William Forist (Forist was later arraigned by the churchwardens for spending Sunday in a tavern). The cloth industry was represented by a fuller and the craftsman who racked his cloth, two weavers and a glover. Roger Loope, the Catholic, was an apothecary and there were two fishermen who made a living netting the Stour and Allen. Some found more precarious employment, like the 'hermit' who lived in the George Inn in the Cornmarket and eked out a living laying gravel in the market.

As the town gradually expanded and new houses rose round the minster, the need for building materials increased. Stone was carted in from Chilmark. Purbeck stone was burnt to make lime, and the records mention the payment of 4d. for oyster shells to help make mortar. Carriers' carts

A drawing of Peter Cox's ½d. trade token of 1667. The obverse describes Cox as a 'Wimborn' feltmaker.

trundled to and fro, adding their din to the noise of the shopkeepers and pedlars crying their wares. Even heavy loads such as Mendip lead were brought in by the indispensable carrier, and their importance is proved by the ½d. trade token issued by John King in 1669, for stamped on the tiny coin is a picture of a horse drawing a covered cart.

By the 1660s no less than twelve Wimborne merchants were producing their own tokens as small change, either valued at ¼d. or ½d. Amongst those for whom an occupation is recorded are the following: Peter Cox (feltmaker), William Easton (linen-weaver), John Anstey (mercer), John Farr (glover), Jeferry Budden (weaver).

In the latter years of the 17th century a shalloon manufactory was established in Redcotts.[36] Shalloon was a closely woven cloth used mainly for linings, and the manufactory was reputed to be the only one in England. Both the employers and the majority of the workforce were Dissenters and, as a 1s. fine was levied against them for failing to attend church, they were eventually forced to seek a town more tolerant of Nonconformity. The business moved to Romsey, depriving Wimborne of a major source of income at a time when it badly needed to attract more employment.

The town's inns and taverns flavoured its social life and offered board and a bed to its visitors. The Crown was the largest, but the George was the most popular, perhaps because its position in the Cornmarket made it a convenient meeting place. Outside its doors stood the stocks where brawlers and drunkards were pelted with filth and rotten fruit: the pillory was probably in Pillory Street, now part of West Borough. Other inns were the King's Arms, the Greyhound and the New Inn, which stood in the Square and had its own bowling green.

The largest of these inns would have had inner courtyards with balconies, from which travelling players and jugglers entertained the crowds. Despite their concern for the future, Wimburnians still found time for pleasure. One ancient custom that had endured was the sale of the 'Church Cakes', baked on behalf of the church and then carried ceremoniously through the streets before being sold throughout the parish by the 'wife of the town' and the 'wife of the country.' Another pastime yet to become extinct was cockfighting. Despite its cruelty, the sport was regularly practiced every Shrove

The town stocks. They once stood in the Cornmarket and are now displayed in the garden of the Priest's House Museum.

The Coach and Horses Inn on the Poole Road in about 1900.

Tuesday by the boys of the Grammar School under the supervision of the schoolmaster. Victory was no hollow crown, for the owner of the winning cock was excused all beatings throughout Lent.

The town's fortunes continued to fluctuate throughout both the 16th and 17th centuries, causing widespread poverty. In 1601 all the various acts and provisions for dealing with the poor were united and made permanent by act of parliament. The result was the Poor Law, a law that was to affect Wimborne and the surrounding villages until well into the 19th century.

To some extent the poor were helped by alms and provisions made in wills for their relief. But the generosity of individuals could not bring poverty to a halt, and a few people created more lasting provision through the foundation of charities. This was not a new approach to the problem, but it does hint at the success of the charities as a means of caring for the sick, the old and the poor. Even the medieval hospital of St Margaret and St Anthony continued to benefit. In 1561, Thomas Boxley left it one acre of land in Rowlands.[37] In addition he left part of a meadow called Rushleys, the income of which was to be devoted to the relief of the poor. It was rather inadequately administered, and in 1830 the Charity Commissioners recommended that in future the trustees should meet annually to discuss how the proceeds could best be applied.

Another charity was that established by Gertrude, Marchioness of Exeter, who by her will dated 1557 left instructions to Sir James Blount to erect within two years of her death almshouses in the parish of Wimborne for six poor men and women. The almshouses were built in what is today Dean's Court Lane and provided with a master or governor. Lady Gertrude was a member of the Blount family, and the endowment for these houses came from land at Little Canford, where the Blounts owned the estate. The almshouses continued to be supported by a succession of owners of Canford, and at the end of the 18th century an annual payment of £2 12s. was available to each of the six inmates. By then Sir John Webb was owner of Canford, and it was he who annually sent into Wimborne half a bull and 40 loaves of bread for distribution to the poor.

A number of other charitable bequests were made in the 17th century. In 1617 Mary Gundry left a yearly rent of £2 to the poor, with the one provision that they should be honest and 'fear God.' Thomas Lyne's Charity of 1621 established a place at Oxford or Cambridge for a scholar from the Grammar School as long as no suitable candidates could be found at Ringwood School.

Collett's Charity was also established in 1621, but once again those who hoped to benefit had to meet certain provisions. The endowment came from land, mostly near Corfe Castle, and the trustees were appointed to pay the proceeds to ten poor persons of Wimborne, five of each sex. The money was distributed on the four principal feast days, i.e. Lady Day, Midsummer Day, Michaelmas and Christmas Day. To be eligible, the poor had to be 'of good and honest fame,' have been 'painful' and honest labourers, and to have borne no illegitimate children. Once having qualified, they had to attend church on Sundays, holy days, Wednesdays and Saturdays in both morning and afternoon unless, of course, too weak or ill to do so.

Three other small charities were established in the 17th century: Alice Brown's (1637), giving £1 to the poor of Wimborne; Richard Habgood's (1642), also for the poor of Wimborne; and Edith Hall's (1683), whose will devised two buildings in the High Street for the benefit of the poor.

The fourth charity founded during the 17th century is arguably the most interesting. It was established by Roger Gillingham, a successful merchant and native of Cowgrove, who by his will dated July 1695 gave the rent from much of his land for the maintenance of an almshouse for four poor men and four poor women and a school for the local children. Gillingham also provided a sum of up to £400 for the purchase of a piece of land next to Pamphill Green. On this was to be built a 'convenient school house with a chamber over it for a schoolmaster to reside in,' and, on either side adjoining the school-house, single-storied accommodation for the eight beneficaries. The whole building was to be constructed of brick and timber with a tiled roof. The results remain visible today, for both the almshouses and school still stand on the edge of the Green, and a stone tablet above the doorway records the 'pious and charitable gift of Roger Gillingham of the Middle Temple.'

To be eligible, the almsfolk had to be at least fifty-five years of age and two of the men and two of the women had to be selected from the poorest people in Cowgrove; the remaining four came from the immediately adjoining tithings. The school had to be capable of accommodating 40 boys drawn from the west of the town from between the Rivers Allen and Stour. The schoolmaster, who had to be single, was obliged to read a chapter from the New Testament to a gathering of both the scholars and the almsfolk twice a day, at eleven in the morning and again at five in the afternoon. The

Roger Gillingham's Almshouses and School on Pamphill Green.

The 1698 tablet commemorating the foundation of Pamphill School and Gillingham's Almshouses. It reads: 'To God & ye poor. The pious & Charitable gift of Roger Gillingham of the Middle Temple, London, Esq. This free Writing School & ye Alms houses adjoining were built by Aldrich Swain, Clerk & Rector of Kington magna in this County & one of the Ministers of this Parish & Persuant to the Gift & trust of the Sayd Roger Gillingham.'

total endowment was £65 a year, of which £20 was paid to the schoolmaster (a high salary for such a post at the time); the balance was divided between the eight almsfolk or used for maintaining the buildings.

After the Reformation responsibility for the maintenance and care of the minster was placed with the churchwardens. The funds for this purpose arose from rents on the fairs at Pamphill and Wimborne, from market dues, from rents from shops in the town and several other properties. Some money was even derived from the letting out of brewing utensils, called brewing leads. The Church Ale, the annual street celebration that originated in the Middle Ages, also helped fill the minsters coffers. Other money came from bequests, sometimes in cash and sometimes in kind, as when livestock or furniture were given for sale. The gift boxes in the minster were another source of profit, and the records mention some of the coins that were found in the boxes when they were emptied: golden royals, French crowns, double and single duckets.[38]

In 1608 the minster's income was extended by the Church Rate, a system of rating on the parishioners that in its first year of operation alone netted over £400.

In combination, this income was used to pay for a whole range of repairs and improvements. One continual source of expense was the bells. Ropes had to be replaced, the clappers and bell wheels repaired. When the bells cracked they had to be taken down and recast. There is some indication that a method of casting using wax was employed (the lost wax process), for when William Horne was engaged to cast a bell in 1506 he was simultaneously supplied with wax. If this is the case, it is amongst the earliest examples of the use of the process. Horne was paid over £4 for his work, but other founders were also brought in, amongst them John Wallis of Salisbury who in 1616 recast the Little Bell.[39]

The 17th century had begun disastrously for the minster. In 1600 the central spire collapsed, destroying part of the chancel as it fell. Thomas Gerard later described what happened: '(the choire beeing then full of people at tenne of clock service, allsoe the streets by reason of the market), a sudden mist ariseing, all the spire steeple, being of a verie great height, was stranglie cast down, the stones battered all the lead and brake much of the timber of the roofe of the church, yet without anie hurt to the people.'[40]

The churchwardens may well have been secretly relieved, for over the years the spire had been a constant source of concern. It was badly damaged during the great gale of November 1530 which lifted most of the lead from the church roof. In 1548 a mason was paid £20 to repair it, and in 1571 7 tons of Chilmark stone were cut and hoisted into place to help keep it upright. The reasons for its final collapse remain unknown, but the tower had never been intended to take the load and it seems probable that a combination of defective masonry and bad design were to blame.

Nor was the interior of the minster in a better state of repair. Eleven years later, when rain seeped into the south side, it was claimed that the 'church stinks like a pigsty.'[41]

The collapse of the spire was only the first of three catastrophes that Wimborne endured during the 17th century. The second was the most traumatic, for in 1638 plague broke out in the town. To imagine the scenes that took place whilst the epidemic raged is impossible, but we can be certain that there was panic, that mobs roamed the streets, that chaos surrendered to drunkenness and despair as the casualty figures mounted. By the time it was over, more than 400 people had died and been buried in common graves in the derelict St Peter's churchyard in the Square. The results of this holocaust were far-reaching, for it led to a gradual decline in the cloth trade. By the start of the 18th century, the merchants and clothiers had departed and the town's main industry was knitting.

The third event to trouble the town was the Civil War. It began in 1642, when the shaken townsfolk were still picking up the pieces in the wake of the plague. Fortunately, the town was spared close involvement in the conflict, but its sympathies lay with Charles I − providing a sharp contrast with neighbouring Poole which remained staunchly Parliamentarian throughout the war. Yet the war did not pass unnoticed. The minster crypt became a stable, windows were broken, and the organ may well have been destroyed so that the pipes could be used for making bullets.

The rising of the Clubmen in Dorset also had no impact on Wimborne, and both town and parish passed unwillingly into the Commonwealth. The new order soon made its mark. The system of ministers was abandoned, only one remaining to serve the entire parish. From 1641 to 1662 the Royal Peculiar Court ceased to operate. The king's arms in the minster were obliterated at a cost of 2s. 6d., the font was replaced by a basin, and the stained glass depicting the royal arms was removed from its window.

An annual charge was made on the revenues of the Corporation from 1647, but a successful petition stating that they were likely to bring both minster and school into disrepair, 'to the great decay of learning and preachinge', led to their eventual remission.

Royalist Wimborne must have found it hard to adapt to the constraints imposed during the Interregnum. Puritan intolerance had no time for the more visible trappings of wealth or pleasure, and it is a pity that we know so little about what took place in the town during the years leading up to the Restoration in 1660. But Wimburnians obviously had a talent for hiding their loyalties. Those who rang the bells to celebrate Cromwell's escape from assassination in 1657 were paid 2s. to buy beer, a sum that was doubled when the bells welcomed Charles II's entry into the town in 1666.[42]

SIX

The Years of Transition

The Restoration might have marked a revival in Wimborne's fortunes, the opening of a new chapter in its history. But the hoped for revival did not take place, and the 18th century was to be one of transition, of hesitant steps forward marred by uncertainty and a decline in trade. It is perhaps apt that the first year for which records have survived of the Wimborne Poor Law rating is 1700, for as the century passed, so also did the Poor Law affect an increasing number of lives. The century was one of paradox. The Wimborne that has survived from the period evokes elegance and wealth. But the wealth was enjoyed by only a handful of its residents, and as the town grew slowly more prosperous the gulf between the rich and the poor gradually widened.

The Poor Law was levied five times a year to provide funds for the relief of the poor, and the money raised was distributed by four elected overseers operating in conjunction with the churchwardens. In 1700 it yielded a gross income of £364, and by the end of the century both income and expenditure had eclipsed the £4,000 mark (See Appendix, Table IV). The rates span the entire century, producing a pattern reflected in both the town's prosperity and its population. From about 1760 onwards the population increased whilst the amount of available work remained static, hence the greater demand on the Poor Rate to relieve the poverty caused by unemployment.

The figures are complex and unwieldy, but the endless lists of payments recorded by the overseers disguise a portrait of the parish that is always revealing, and often tells us much about the lives of those who lived in the town. Nor were strangers ignored. Mary Piercy, a soldier's widow with four children, was given 3s. when passing through Wimborne bound for Penzance in the spring of 1737.[1] Such travellers were issued with passes to enable them to obtain relief without being mistaken for beggars, for begging was then a punishable offence.

Many of these payments to travellers marked an attempt by the overseers to hurry their departure from the town. Demands for money were constant, and ranged from the cost of inoculation against smallpox to the maintenance of the widowed and the provision of midwives. Amounts varied to meet particular needs, but the standard payment to the 'impotent poor', as they were called, was 1s. a week.

One of the more positive ways adopted by the overseers to ease the burden on the rates was the apprenticing out of children as soon as they were old enough to work, which often was when they were as young as seven. The young apprentices were given new clothes at parish expense before joining their masters. In 1703 the list of clothing included petticoats and waistcoats given to the 'children that are bound out Apprentice.'[2]

The developing Newfoundland trade also provided opportunities for

employment, as the following account shows:

24th March 1714. Paid for Forrist's Boy att his going to Newfoundland, 2 neckclothes, a Sea Ring, 2 hatts, a chest, Lock, staples, making his bed sack, and blew shirt, and for a comb, and in our Expences in putting him out ... 12s.[3]

Two other entries in the accounts, dated January and June in the preceding year, suggest the reasons for young Forrist's departure. The first records the payment of 12s. to Ann Harvey for spending seventeen days with Mary Forrist when she was lying-in following the birth of a child.[4] The second reveals a tragedy that was typical of the age.

> 17th June 1713
> Paid Samuel Colborne to looking to goody Forrist, 15s.
> Paid for the Minister's and Clarkes fees for burying goody fforist, 1s. 1d.
> Paid for her grave, 1s.
> Paid for beer and biskett for those that carryed her, 4s. 6d.
> Paid for her coffin, 7s.
> Paid for tending her in her sickness to Piddel's wife, 3s.
> Paid goody Chipley for help laying her forth, 6s 6d.[5]

'Goody' Mary Forrist had died within six months of the birth of her child, forcing the overseers to find employment for her now motherless son.

The care of orphans was a duty that the overseers could not avoid, but when the children were illegitimate every effort was made to find the father so that he could be made to reimburse the parish for its expenses. The courts record a number of single pregnant women who had been required, under oath, to state the name and whereabouts of the reputed father.

Once such case concerned Mary, wife of a sailor, Richard White, and her evidence gives a clear insight into several aspects of social and moral life in mid-18th century Wimborne. She was examined before the justices in 1768 and stated that she had not seen her husband for eighteen years. She went on to admit that she had given birth to an illegitimate daughter, who had since become chargeable to the parish. She also admitted that on first discovering her pregnancy she had approached the father, James Percy, a Wimborne stone mason and timber merchant, and told him of her condition. Self-interest added to Percy's dismay, and he told her that 'he would not have it happened for an Hundred Pounds.' He went on to promise that 'if she would drink a draft that he would bring her, He, the said James Percy, would keep her like a Gentlewoman.' Mary was not fooled, saying 'she had committed sin enough already, and would add no more to it ...'[6]

Percy was a member of a well-known Wimborne family, and anxious to conceal his complicity by attempting to procure an abortion. Perhaps his youth and inexperience, he was only seventeen or eighteen at the time, led him to make claims than in his maturity he would have scorned. Or perhaps I am being charitable? In August 1769 he fathered a second illegitimate child, on another woman, and his failure to pay maintenance led to his imprisonment in Dorchester.[7] In December 1770 the parish paid 5s. for the grave and coffin of this second child. Percy lies buried in a tomb, that still survives, to the south of the minster.

To assist them in their work, the overseers were helped by a parish constable elected by the manorial courts. Various offences such as begging, vagrancy and the failure to pay maintenance could lead to an appearance in court — and eventual imprisonment in Dorchester. But the magistrates had

King Street. The upper illustration shows the 17th and 18th century cottages on the north side of the street that were demolished in the 1950s. The lower photograph shows the minster car park that now occupies their site. Beyond stands the former National School, now the Ferndown and Wimborne Teachers' Centre.

Matthew Percy in 1747.

The Percy family tomb, to the south of the minster. The tomb is one of the few surviving funerary monuments and marks the resting place of both Matthew and James Percy, noted Wimborne merchants and tradesmen.

The tomb of Anthony Ettrick, and one of the Minster Church's most remarkable curiosities. Ettrick, who was born in 1623, became convinced that he would die on attaining the biblically allotted span of 'three score years and ten.' In fact he survived for a further decade, and the premature date of 1693 on his tomb chest had to be amended to 1703. Ettrick's family seat was at Holt Lodge, and as a lawyer and Recorder of Poole he was an influential local figure. Legend records that in a fit of pique he vowed not to be buried in the minster or outside it, nor above ground nor below it; hence his curious resting place as the 'man in the wall.'

other options, like the town 'blind house' or lock-up, the stocks, pillory, and the ducking stool overlooking the River Allen used for scolds and scandal-mongers. The stocks remained in use until at least 1835, for it was then that a Richard Cox was placed in them for three hours. Other punishments were more savage. In 1724 a gipsy girl was brought before the magistrates for robbery, an offence for which she was sentenced to a public whipping.[8]

Another of the tasks confronting the overseers was 'removal', the eviction from the town to the parish of their birth of all those who sought relief and rented property at less than £10 a year. Towns as distant as Bristol and Llanderryn in Glamorgan are all mentioned as having provided Wimborne with paupers who were later sent back to their parishes.

There were literally hundreds of such cases, but that of Robert Hiscock of Hampreston illustrates the difficulties faced by the poor. Hiscock had made a prudent marriage (or so it must have seemed) to Mary Buffett of Wimborne. On marriage he was entitled to a 'little leasehold cottage situate at or near Leigh Common.' The cottage had passed to his wife through her grandfather, who had granted her the property for the remainder of a 99 year lease at a rent of 6d. payable to the lord of the manor, Sir William Hanham. Robert and Mary Hiscock had seven children, but by the date of Hiscock's application for poor relief in 1768 only one remained at home, the rest having found jobs as servants. Following his application, Hiscock was told that he was not entitled to remain in Wimborne and would have to return to Hampreston for relief — a legal technicality that forced the Hiscocks' to leave their cottage.[9]

One of the major results of 18th century Poor Law administration in Wimborne was the construction of the workhouse. The decision was made after a meeting in 1750. A week later it was reported that a parcel of land with a tenement belonging to an Elizabeth Raven could be bought for £160.[10] A committee was then formed to run the workhouse, comprising John Bankes of Kingston Lacy, Henry Fitch of High Hall, Nicholas Russell, Richard Wright, Christopher King, David Lambert, Thomas Oakley, John Fryer, Leonard Martin, Richard Tory, William Batt and

Matthew Raindle – all of whom were local landowners or wealthy tradesmen and farmers.

The notion of building the workhouse coincided with the first major increase in poor relief expenditure. Its promoters initially seem to have thought of it as virtually self-supporting: the inmates, selected from the poorest members of the community, were to be engaged in manufacture, and the sale of their produce was to meet the expense of their keep. The master appointed to have charge of the house was to be 'well skilled both in linnen and woollen manufactures and also accounts,' but its inmates appear to have been employed in making watch chains and the throwing of silk for the Sherborne mills. The first master was William Nothoor at an annual £14 salary, and a doctor was appointed to look after the health of the inmates – his duties also including 'both physic and surgery for such Poor as shall be sent to him by the Parish Officer.'

Following the appointment of a succession of masters, in 1784 the committee decided that the workhouse should be let out to a contractor who in return would pay 1s. 9d. per head per week for a term of one year. The first contractor was Richard Mitchell who was instructed to 'find and provide the Poor with Meat, Drink, Clothing and all other Necessaries.'[11] It was also decided that a matron was required. A Mrs Phillips was appointed, and such was her efficiency that in 1794 and 1797 she was paid a bonus of two guineas in addition to her salary.

The workhouse stood on the east side of East Borough on a plot of land adjoining the house of the Castleman family (rebuilt by them in 1823 and now Allendale). Its closeness to so substantial a house soon led to complaints that the 'necessary houses' (lavatories) were 'a great nuisance', and they were quickly moved to the opposite corner of the grounds so that the effluent could go straight into the River Allen.[12]

The operation of the Poor Law represented an important influence on life in 18th century Wimborne. Its work also embraced the payment of county rates towards the maintenance of bridges, infirmaries, prisons and asylums, making it a form of local government that involved all the most influential members of the parish community. The work done by the overseers won them few friends, but it was unremitting and often emotionally exhausting.

The workhouse door. Note the studs, the gas lamp and the Sun Fire Insurance mark.

Allen Court, East Borough, once the site of the workhouse.

Allendale House, built by the Castleman family in 1823. By 1900 it was a private school, since then it has been the offices of Wimborne Council and it is now an antique shop. What were originally its pleasure gardens running down to the Allen are now the site of the Allendale Community Centre and a car park.

Occasionally their labours were rewarded, as in 1769 when the out-going overseers were each paid £17 'for the care and Great trouble they have been at in doing parish business.'[13] Not all were such faithful servants to their parish. In 1818 George Scott, a former overseer, was threatened with prosecution for corruption, but the charge was dropped for lack of evidence. Scott's guilt seems certain, for a little later he refunded £50 to the parish.[14]

Another vital link in the chain by which Wimborne was governed were the manorial courts. They were run by the Hanham family based at Dean's Court, and by the 18th century they had two primary functions: one was the administration of the affairs in the manor (which included a substantial part of the town as well as some outlying land), the other was controlling the properties that belonged to the Deanery.[15]

The courts met twice a year, and they were presided over by a legally qualified steward who represented the interests of the Hanhams. Below him was the bailiff who dealt with the running of the court. Membership of the court comprised all who rented Deanery property, and it was they who elected the officers responsible for carrying out the court's orders within the Deanery estates. Amongst the officers were two constables, two portreeves, two aletasters, two searchers and sealers of leather, and two haywards.

The job of the constables and aletasters is self-explanatory: the former kept the peace, the latter tested the quality of the beers brewed in the town. The searchers and sealers of leather inspected all goods made out of leather, marking each piece with a seal if it passed inspection. The haywards hint at the continued importance of farming in the life of the town. Pigs still grubbed and foraged in the churchyard. Livestock found wandering untended through the streets was taken by the hayward to the town pound, which was situated near the Green Man public house. Many of these officers also served as overseers and churchwardens, adding to their powers.

The court's interests were considerable. In 1724 they ordered the owner of a gravel pit, partly filled with water, to fence it before a child was drowned. In 1748 the constables turned their attentions to the lodging houses of Joseph Blake and the widow, Elizabeth Brown, in which were 'great numbers of stroleing Beggars and other disorderly persons', and both were fined 10s. A few years later six tradesmen were presented for selling by short weights, and in 1813 the portreeve was ordered to appear before the court to give information against a baker who had been selling short weight loaves. On another occasion the aletasters reported a beer shop proprietor, 'living within the parish,' who refused to allow them to inspect his ale.

The court officers themselves were not always above reproach. In 1794 a former portreeve, Thomas Street, was presented for failing to return his brass weights and a gallon measure to the court on the termination of his period of office. He had also retained 'the Portreeve's Gown and Cloak, one Silver Laced hat and the Mace' − a list that evokes the official uniform worn by the officers.

Roads, footpaths and watercourses were another cause of concern to the court. In 1722 it ordered the construction of a foot-bridge over a street channel so that the townsfolk could carry their dead to the minster graveyard. When the road leading from 'Mr Henwood's Corner' to Redcotts Gate was in need of repair, they ordered the supervisors of the

58

A notice enforcing market tolls in accordance with the authority of the Deanery Court and dated 1807.

Wimborne, 17 *August,* 1807.

NOTICE is hereby given, that if any Persons fhall hereafter expofe to Sale, in the Market of this Town, any of the Articles undermentioned; and fhall refufe, or neglect to pay, to JAMES CLUETT, the renter of the faid Market, the feveral ancient and accuftomed Tolls fet oppofite to the fame; the defaulters will be profecuted.   By order of the Rev. Sir JAMES HANHAM, Bart. the Owner of the faid Market.

W. CASTLEMAN,
STEWARD.

TOLLS.

	s.	d.
For every Head of Black Cattle - - - - - - - - - - - - -		1
For every Pig - - - - - - - - - - - - - - - - - - -		½
For every Score of Sheep, and so in proportion for a less number - -	1	
For every Person Hawking or Selling any Commodity, each time - -		1

highway to re-gravel it, backed by the threat of a fine. The parish roads suffered the normal wear and tear that followed constant use by livestock and waggons. But some evidently regarded gravelled roads as a private source of ballast. Early in the century two men were discovered digging gravel from a road at Colehill and were accused of being a 'nuisance to the King's Highway.'

Another irritation that plagued the 18th century town as much as it does now was parking. Eventually a general prohibition was issued forbidding waggons and carts to be left 'in the Streets and Lanes of the town at night under a penalty of 18s.' The penalty was severe, nearly the equivalent of two weeks' wages for a carter.

The manorial courts were also responsible for the state of the buildings in the town. Even such obvious things as loose bricks and tiles which presented a hazard to passers-by were their concern. In 1721 a John Barnes was ordered to repair his house because it constituted a danger to men and horses passing beneath it. Three years later Oliver Rowden's chimney flue, sited against the back of the Bell Inn, was reported as dangerous and he was

A view of Cowgrove and Pamphill
from the Stour valley. The
building on the extreme left is the
former Court House.

ordered to either pull it down or repair it within a month. Even the lord of the manor was not immune to being presented in his own court for failure to maintain his property, as in 1784 when some of the Hanham's buildings in Cook Row were reported to be so much out of repair as to be dangerous.

The town's mills also required the occasional support of the courts to keep them turning. There were three mills within the town on the River Allen, a paper mill situated nearly opposite the Coach and Horses, and two for grinding corn, Walford and the Town Mill. It was imperative that the water flow to these mills should not be hindered, and the courts often had to order those living alongside the stream to clear it of weeds and rubbish.

In 1772 *The London Directory* announced the departure of a regular coach service to Wimborne at a cost of £1. 4s. The journey took about fourteen hours – 'If God permits' and not brought to a premature halt by the highwaymen hiding in the New Forest. By the end of the century the service had been extended, to Exeter, Bath, Salisbury and Bristol.

Despite the unemployment, Wimborne was surviving. Its geographical position between the Allen and Stour made it a natural focal point for roads and bridges. With Poole so close, it was also eminently suited to act as an inland staging-post for the coastal trade and the neighbouring market towns of Cranborne, Ringwood and Blandford. Earlier in the century, a series of roads based on a system of tolls had gradually spread throughout the country. They were known as turnpikes and, in order to benefit from their development, a group of enterprising citizens from Wimborne and Poole had obtained a parliamentary act in 1755 authorizing the construction of a good quality turnpike from Poole to Cranborne, via Wimborne.[16]

The Crown and Anchor being demolished. The inn was originally called The Case is Altered and stood on or near the site of the turnpike tollhouse. The present Crown and Anchor is a modern building.

The turnpike tollhouse and gate on the Wimborne-Blandford turnpike road in about 1860. St Margaret's Almshouse chapel stands behind the tollhouse. The road to the right went towards Hillbutts and Kingston Lacy.

Three years later the Ringwood, Longham and Leigh Turnpike was opened, providing an eastward link with London via Ringwood and Southampton. The westward link with Blandford was first forged through a junction with the Wimborne-Poole turnpike in Corfe Mullen, but in 1765 a direct turnpike was authorized between the two towns. The road ran from Pye Corner at the junction of King Street and West Street to St Margaret's Almshouse, and then through Stone, Cowgrove and Kingston Lacy along the valley of the Stour into Blandford. The last of the Wimborne turnpikes, that going over Julian's Bridge, through Corfe Mullen and on to Dorchester via Charborough (roughly the A31), was not established until 1841.

Toll-houses were erected at key points along the length of the turnpikes. In 1822 the toll-house at Walford Bridge (very close to the present Crown & Anchor Inn) collected a total of £162. Not all were profitable. In 1853 the Blandford and Wimborne Turnpike still owed £1,800 and its income of £241 was only £29 more than its expenditure. Perhaps inevitably, some of the keepers who rented the toll-houses must have felt that they were unlikely to make a living: one keeper, at the Ringwood Gate, even absconded with £12 worth of tolls.

The turnpikes brought mixed blessings. The working population was legally liable to spend six days a year helping construct or repair them. They also added to the cost of maintaining the town's bridges. East Brook Bridge had to be widened by eight feet. A new bridge was built at Honeybrook on the road to Cranborne in 1784 at a cost of over £11. In one year alone, 1802, £255 was spent on repairs to Walford and Julian's Bridges. So concerned were the townsfolk about the state of Canford Bridge that a committee was even appointed to prepare a report on its condition.[18] In 1793 it was rebuilt and its twelve medieval arches were reduced to three over the river.

Another burden that fell on the turnpike trustees was the cost of clearing the draining channels, or canals, that ran through East and West Boroughs and discharged into the Allen near Walford Bridge.[19] They had been dug in 1762, ostensibly to provide water for fire-fighting and street-cleaning, but many found them a convenient place for dumping refuse and they often flooded, blocking the northern entrance into the town.

The digging of the canals is indicative of the threat still posed by fire in the 18th century town. Most houses were still thatched, and the church-wardens kept fire-crooks in the minster vestry and porch for pulling burning

Walford Bridge looking north, with the old Crown and Anchor on the left.

*Pamphill Forge in the early 1920s.
Frank Budden (on the right) was
general smithy to the Kingston
Lacy estate.*

thatch from roofs. But the town needed more than such primitive equipment, and in 1761 it was decided to purchase a proper fire-engine – 'to work by suction and a constant stream with seven foot of suction pipe & two lengths of leather pipe (with brass screws) containing forty feet each.'[20] It was bought from John Broadbent, 'Engine Maker in Piccadilly', at a cost of £32. 10s., and such was its importance that it was kept in the west tower of the minster. Its arrival was timely, for in the following year Wareham was swept by fire and the churchwardens, perhaps grateful that Wimborne had been spared, paid out over £1 in bread to 'the people of Wareham.'[21] Wareham's destruction also served as a warning, for in its wake the Wimborne churchwardens ordered all bakers and blacksmiths to tile their roofs. They also insisted that no ricks of faggots be kept in the town and made shopkeepers reduce the amount of fuel stored on their premises.

The fire risks in Wimborne were considerable. As well as the bakers and blacksmiths, there were three chandlers making soap and candles. Some tradesmen even insured against fire, and there still is a Sun Fire Insurance plaque which probably dates from the 1770s on a house in the Cornmarket.

Wimborne's shopkeepers appear to have successfully survived the decline in trade, adding to the air of self-sufficiency that had always characterized the town. There were grocers who dealt in snuff, hops and lamp-oil; seedsmen who supplied liquor and lead. Others offered almanacks and brooms and yet managed to combine shopkeeping with the less pleasant occupations of slaughterer and chimney-sweep. There were cobblers, tailors and coopers, as well as shroud and coffin makers and a number of carpenters. A Mrs Walker made stays for women's dresses. A Mr Braffett supplied knitting needles and spades. The town had its own barber, who also acted as its dentist.[22]

Despite the departure of the cloth trade, a trade directory of 1792 claimed that Wimborne was 'chiefly maintained by a woollen manufactory.'[23] In reality it was a cottage industry that extended throughout the parish. It gave work to many families, who supplemented their income producing woollen stockings, for which they received 1s. a pair.

A view of some 17th century town houses in the Cornmarket, since demolished but once typical of houses in Wimborne.

One trade in Wimborne that flourished throughout the century was smuggling. The town was close to both Christchurch and Poole and many of the townsfolk played their part in the landing and sale of contraband. The King's Arms was the headquarters of the local excise officers, but their presence made little difference to the nocturnal activities of the smuggling gangs, and the battle of wits between smuggler and exciseman continued until well into the 19th century. The area's most notorious smuggler was Isaac Gulliver, now remembered as a rich source of unlikely legends — of which the most popular (that he was pardoned for revealing a plot to murder George III) is not borne out by the facts. Gulliver later claimed that no one had died as a result of his activities, and in 1782 he took advantage of a free pardon to smugglers and settled in West Borough, becoming a legitimate businessman. His daughter made an astute marriage to William Fryer (principal partner in the town's first country bank, established in about 1789).[24] Gulliver himself became a respected churchwarden, and when he died in 1822 his burial took place in the nave aisle of the minster.[25]

Men like Gulliver added colour to the 18th century town. But the parish could boast other 'characters', and perhaps the best known to his contemporaries was Benjamin Bower of Holt who at over 34 stone was reputed to be the heaviest man in England. Bower died as he had lived. In 1763, in an attempt to ward off the gout, he downed a gallon of cider at a single draught and promptly fell dead on the floor. Such was his size, bricklayers had to knock down part of the tavern in which he had died in order to remove him for burial.

In the early 18th century a visitor to Wimborne wrote: 'The town has little reason to boast either of the cleanliness of its streets, or the neatness and regularity of its buildings.'

The uncleanliness continued, but by 1800 much of the town had been rebuilt, providing the elegant air of genteel prosperity that still survives in some of Wimborne's architecture. The best of Wimborne's taverns became coaching inns offering 'stabling and well-ventilated laundry.' Their rooms were enlarged, providing space for dances and recitals. Georgian town

18th century cottages in East Borough. These thatched cottages survived the 1864 fire. Note the large gutter running on brackets beneath the semi-dormer windows.

houses gradually replaced the timber-framing and wattle and daub. The Market House in the Cornmarket dates from 1758. The redundant Tivoli Cinema in West Borough conceals the remains of a Georgian facade. The present Conservative Club and the buildings between it and the Square all belong to the 18th century. Dean's Court was rebuilt in 1725 by Sir William Hanham, and by the time the work had been finished the core of the medieval deanery had been enclosed by an 'L' shaped building which surrounded it to the north and east. (In 1868 the medieval hall was demolished, and no part of the ancient deanery now survives above ground level).[26]

In the rural parish the pattern was much the same. High Hall, the fine 17th century home of the Fitch family, was modified in the 18th — as was the Manor House on Pamphill Green. The interior of Kingston Lacy, home of the Bankes family and finished in 1665, was largely refurbished.

The modifications to older buildings and the construction of new, airy and spacious houses gave scope to a much wider range of furnishings, the hanging of paintings on walls, the use of wall-papers and curtains, the space needed for clocks, sculpted figures, larger tables and sideboards. Harpsichords found a place in any house whose occupants aspired to 'society.'

By the end of the century 'society' had become all-important, forming divisions between the classes that had been unknown in Tudor Wimborne. Families like the Hanhams, Bankes, Fitches, Glyns and Sturts provided a style and elegance that others could only imitate. Hunting, balls and dinners filled their annual calendars. Coaches carried them and their friends on an interminable round of exchange visits from country house to country house, giving employment to Wimborne's first coachmaker, Robert Hart.

The well-to-do farmers, the professional men and wealthier tradesmen in the town followed in the steps of the gentry. They copied their clothing and furnishings, their daughters learnt 'decorum' and music, their sons were educated at the Grammar School, and they mixed with the gentry at functions in the town. Fashionable society was reliant on doctors and lawyers for guarding its health and arranging its affairs. Gradually the professional classes settled in the town, and by the end of the century Wimborne boasted no fewer than seven attorneys.[27]

It would be misleading to depict the gentry as idle seekers after pleasure, for many participated in the life of the town, encouraging improvements and lending their name and their wealth to causes in need of support. John Bankes, who died in 1714, had been an M.P. for Corfe Castle; two of his sons, the eldest John, and Henry, became barristers and politicians. Henry married twice, his second wife providing the estate with an heir and adding to its already considerable wealth. The son of this marriage, another Henry (1757-1834), was Corfe's M.P. for forty-seven years, but he also took an interest in Wimborne, involving himself in the running of the workhouse and serving as an Official of the Royal Peculiar for nearly thirty years.[28]

The Hanhams also played their part in Wimborne's life. Members of the family had promoted the turnpikes and Sir William (c.1694-1762), a baronet for fifty-three years, was a local magistrate. The same was true of his son, another William, who in due course served as a churchwarden. It is almost impossible to disentangle the two Reverend Sir James Hanhams (1726-1806 and 1760-1849) from the affairs of the town, for both were ministers at the minster.

Hartlands, a fine early 19th century town house in East Borough.

A builder's tablet in King Street. The date reflects the amount of new building that took place in the mid-18th century.

The High Street in 1905. The four-in-hand coach arrived daily from Bournemouth.

Whilst Wimborne gradually mellowed into a tranquil country town, life in the surrounding countryside went on as before. The farming calendar was not affected by the whims of fashion. The eighteenth century farm was still very similar to its 17th century counterpart, and John Jay's farm at Leigh, though examined in 1640, was probably still typical of many of the farms in the parish. It contained 40 acres of wheat and 40 of barley, 30 acres of oats and 10 acres each of pease and vetches; the meadows supplied 20 loads of hay. The livestock totalled 100 ewes, each with a lamb, 20 pigs and 2 colts; poultry consisted of 40 ducks, 30 geese and 20 turkeys. The farm's orchards, then so vital to general farming, yielded 40 bushels of apples and 10 of pears − in addition there were marketable quantities of plums and cherries.[29].

It is probable that by the beginning of the 18th century most farming outside the Kingston Lacy area was carried on in enclosed farms. Kingston Lacy still retained the open common-field system until 1786, when the land was enclosed and divided into separate farms by act of parliament. The land involved totalled 3,000 acres (including two areas of downland, two large common-fields and Pillsmoor and Hinton Moor), but in the Holt section of the estate enclosure merely completed a process that had already begun.[30].

The latter years of the 18th century brought great hardship to many farmers. There was a succession of poor harvests, and many landowners were trying to raise rents on leasehold farms whilst simultaneously shortening the leases. Competition from other parts of the country did not help, as the following report dated 1796 makes all too clear: 'There has been so large a

66

The High Street in the late 1920s. A solitary horse-drawn cart stands outside Rowe's chemist shop. Note how the lofty brick gable of the now demolished Methodist Church vies in height with the minster chancel.

quantity of fine English wheat brought into the port of Poole within these three weeks past (not less than 4,000 quarters) that we flatter ourselves the circumstances cannot fail to bring their stock to market at reduced prices, unless they are disposed rather to throw it on the dunghill...'[31]

In 1836 an act was passed for commuting the payment of tithes in kind for payment in cash. The act required an accurate survey of land and its uses, and the Wimborne parish survey provides us with an excellent portrait of agriculture in the parish. It was surveyed in 1847, when its total acreage of 11,968 was divided as follows:

Arable	5,421	Homesteads & gardens	304
Meadow & pasture	3,178	Heathlands	1,034
Downland	477	Woods & plantations	822
Common lands	496	Buildings	97
Orchards	40	Roads and waste	99

The sum of money for the whole parish payable in lieu of tithes was £2,500 – of which £2,416 was payable to the Corporation of Queen Elizabeth Grammar School. The remainder went to Edward VI Grammar School in Sherborne, who still controlled the 356 acres of Bradford Farm granted to the school by Elizabeth I.[32]

The Tithe Apportionment makes it clear that most of the farms in the parish were leased by tenants: the few owner occupiers owned only the smallest farms. In 1847 the largest farm in Wimborne, King Down Farm, was held by the twenty-seven-year-old Charles Louch, and the farm's 1,191 acres were worked by fifty labourers.

Farm sizes varied considerably. Chilbridge Farm, a creation of the Kingston Lacy enclosures, contained a total of 458 acres: 324 arable, 130 pasture – the balance was occupied by buildings and yards. Of the small to medium sized farms in the Allen valley and the eastern half of the parish there were Petersham Farm, 180 acres and employing nine labourers, and Pig Oak Farm, held by William Holland, containing 200 acres and employing only six labourers, presumably because he was helped by his son and two unmarried daughters.[33] The Allen appears to have acted as a natural divide to the farming in the parish. More corn was grown to its west, and there was a larger proportion of mixed and dairy farming on its eastern bank.

It is worth noticing the ratio of labourers to acreage. For a 200 acre farm to survive today it would need no more than two workers, but its 19th century ancestors gave employment to the entire rural community. Young boys began their careers keeping birds from the growing corn before being initiated into the art of ploughing with horses. At harvest time, wives and families gathered in the fields to bind and stook the sheaves.

A large number of the farms in the parish were scattered and split into small fields. Normally tenant farmers rented their land from a single landlord, but the complex landowning character of the parish led to many exceptions. One farmer, John Raindle, owned nearly half his 136 acres, but the balance was rented from five different landowners in parcels ranging from 2 to 28 acres.[34]

The smaller farms, such as Crooked Withies in Holt, practised as mixed a husbandry as was possible. The farm ran 120 sheep, 9 dairy cows, 3 heifers in calf and 9 pigs, plus a sow with '13 fine shoots.' Potatoes were also grown, and ricks of barley and oats were kept for winter fodder. Many such farms found it difficult to survive, and in the mid-19th century the farm was sold because of declining business.[35]

Other considerations troubled many farmers in the early 19th century. In the autumn of 1830 there were riots throughout much of Dorset over the threat posed to employment by the invention of threshing machines. At one point there was concern that a 'Mob of evil disposed persons' might rampage through Wimborne. But the riot never took place, and the only chance of trouble was provided by a group of rioters calling themselves the 'Handley Torches.'[36] Much of their anger was directed against Mr Castleman, agent and steward to the Bankes estate, and they wrote him a characteristically confused letter threatening to burn his house, 'for you are an inhuman monster and we will dash out your brains – Bankes and your sett aught to be sent to Hell.'[37]

Empty threats did little to help the labourers cause, and the riots failed to improve their conditions. Significant changes in the life of the farm labourer had to wait until after the First World War, and the only slight improvement took place in the years leading up to the agricultural depression of the 1870s. Farmers round Wimborne were spared the worst of the depression. Once again the town's site was its own best ally, for the large and growing markets for agricultural produce in expanding Poole and the new resort of Bournemouth cushioned Wimborne from the worst of its effects.

SEVEN

An English Country Town

According to Wimborne folk-lore, a drunken Grenadier threw himself off the minster tower for a wager during the Napoleonic Wars – and survived. Such bravado, and the Grenadier's miraculous escape, seem almost a reflection of the state of the town at the start of the 19th century. It too had risked much and survived unscathed the changes in its fortunes, and the century that lay ahead was to see it expand beyond recognition and its population double to over 6,000. When Queen Victoria came to the throne in 1837 the minster crypt was under water. The Grammar School had a mere 15 boarders and 25 day-boys. Unmarried women with children in the workhouse were compelled to distinguish themselves from the rest of the inmates by wearing a mob cap and a grey dress of coarse cloth. By the date of Queen Victoria's death in 1901 the minster had been restored, the school was thriving, and the workhouse was little more than half a century from its final demolition.

If any one building symbolizes the enduring character of Wimborne and the surrounding parish it is surely the minster. By the mid-19th century a place of worship had stood in the centre of the town for over 1,000 years. As well as dominating Wimborne's spiritual life and acting as a centre for prayer, it had become the landmark by which the town was recognized and the pulse by which its health could be measured. In 1857 the much-needed restoration was begun. The north and south chapels were extensively rebuilt, and the roofs of both chapels and the chancel were replaced. Internal work led to the removal of the 16th century whitewash. The painting of a crucifixion scene dating from the 13th and 14th centuries in the north transept was uncovered and survives to this day.[1] Other modifications saw the removal of the west gallery and the cast iron pillars that supported it, the first stages in the complete removal of the choir canopies, and the placing of the organ in the south transept.

The Chained Library, which had been founded by the Reverend William Stone in 1686, was fitted with new shelves and rods for attaching the chains. The Library had been added to by successive ministers and men such as Roger Gillingham. But it was not solely for the use of the clergy, indeed Gillingham's bequest of books had stated that they were to be enjoyed by the 'gentry, shopkeepers and the better sort of inhabitants'[2] – by which he probably meant all those who could read.

In 1891 the three-sided 17th century sun-dial (it bears the date 1676 on its main face) was taken from the gable of the south transept during alterations and re-erected on a pillar to the south of the west tower three years later. The organ was also restored. A new organ had been purchased in 1664 for £180 to replace the one destroyed during the Civil War. Despite occasional repairs, it continued to serve the minster for 200 years. In 1865 it was taken

The elaborate stone sun-dial made in 1676 and re-set by the west tower in 1894, following its removal from the gable of the south transept roof.

The chained library in the Minster Church. Most books are shelved with spines to the back of the bookcases so that the chains can be fixed to the opening edge of each book cover.

to London and entirely rebuilt at a cost of £764. It has since been twice rebuilt, re-opening in June 1965 with a special recital.[3]

One further symbol of both the town and the minster is the Quarter Jack, the striking jack in the form of a soldier that stands in the north window of the west tower. It is first mentioned in the churchwardens' accounts of 1662 when a Blandford carpenter was paid 10s. for 'carving the Jack.' Its present appearance dates from the early 19th century when it was repainted in the uniform of a Grenadier as a sign of loyalty during the Napoleonic Wars.

Other churches in the parish were also to benefit from the restoration work carried out in the 19th century. By 1830 the ancient chapel at Holt was so dilapidated it needed to be completely rebuilt. The Wimborne architect, John Tulloch, drew up the plans and the final church, still dedicated to St James, was completed in 1835 with seats for 319 parishioners. Forty years later it was provided with the fine 17th century pulpit that had previously stood in the minster.

By the 1880s the growing population in the parish had accelerated its division into smaller units, both ecclesiastical and civil, and this in turn led to the building of new churches. In 1894 Holt became a civil parish in its own right, and that same year the 5,703 acres of Pamphill were made a parish to the west of Wimborne. The church of St Stephen (reminiscent of the medieval church at Kingston Lacy) was built in 1907 for £4,000 on a site donated by the Bankes family. Colehill became a separate parish in 1896. Its church, completed in the preceding year and dedicated to St Michael, is of particular interest because of the use of red bricks with black and white timber work that make its architecture so unusual.[4] The other ecclesiastical parish to be created in the 19th century is that of New Borough and Leigh, formed in 1876 to cater for those moving into the new houses springing up round the railway station, along Leigh Road and in the developing suburb of Rowlands. Its church was built when the parish was formed, and is dedicated to St John the Evangelist.

Despite the presence of the minster, or perhaps because of it, the 19th century saw the consolidation of Noncomformity in the town. Its early history had been marred by legal constraints and abuse. As early as 1695 land had been given for a Congregational Church,[5] and shortly afterwards a Wimborne gardener left the income from a garden to help pay for a minister.[6] By 1824 its membership had fallen to thirty, and it was only in 1885 that its chapel in Chapel Lane was renovated.

A Methodist preacher had arrived in Wimborne in 1799, but the strength of opposition had halted the establishment of a base in the town.[7] The preaching of John Parsons in a house in West Borough so angered some locals that its windows were broken, forcing him to abandon it and move to Colehill. But attitudes changed, and the greater piety and religious toleration of the period enabled the Methodists to build a church in the Cornmarket in 1820 and make the town the centre for twelve rural chapels, including Broomhill, Holt and Colehill. Their church was soon too small and in 1868 the move to the present site in King Street was made. This church, which had seating for 650, has only recently been demolished and replaced.

By the end of the 19th century both the Plymouth Brethren and Salvation Army had become established in the town. The Salvation Army initially made use of the former Methodist Church in the Cornmarket, but the building later became a Masonic Hall and a temporary cinema.

Only the Catholics have had to wait until the 20th century before returning to the town. Since the Reformation they had been forced to worship in private houses served by itinerant priests, but in 1933 the stone-built church of St Catherine's was finally built in Leigh Road. A tower was added three years later, since when there has always been a resident priest for Wimborne's Catholic community.

The various churches in 19th century Wimborne were easily outnumbered by the skills and crafts that still flourished in the town, and the trade directories of the period reflect the enterprise of its shopkeepers and craftsmen. In 1824 there were 6 bakers, 10 boot and shoe makers, 4 chair makers,

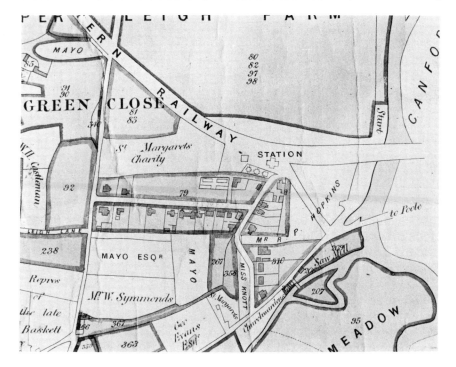

A detail from the Hanham Estate map of 1873 showing the site of the railway station and the housing development taking place in the area.

Cowdry's Bakery on the corner of Prior's Walk and West Borough. The bakery still continues and this photograph, taken in about 1910, shows a building typical of many of Wimborne's plain 18th century small town houses.

3 curriers, 6 linen drapers, 3 saddlers, 6 tailors, as well as surgeons, pawn-brokers, auctioneers, butchers, watch makers, tallow chandlers and the Old Town Brewery — which supplied some of the 14 inns and 4 beer-shops.

There was also the Grammar School, which by the middle of the century was in disarray and a source of endless complaints by the townsfolk. Its problems stemmed from its domination by a group of governors who as local landowners used their influence to pay ridiculous low tithes to the Corporation, making it impossible for the school to develop. The Charity Commissioners found mismanagement wherever they looked. Even the education was suffering, for the constraints imposed on the headmaster limited his freedom to control the curriculum. The school's affairs were examined by the attorney-general's office, who insisted that £4,500 be set aside for rebuilding or repairs to the school. The money was unwisely spent. The school took up temporary residence in the Albion Inn, but its replacement, the large brick building in mock Elizabethan style constructed between 1849 and 1851, was later described by a school inspector as a 'rambling structure with a dark entrance and ill-lighted passages winding around the building.' Only the education improved. The Charity Commissioners instructed the

The staff of the Julian Brewery in 1904.

Corporation to widen the curriculum to include Latin, French, Mathematics, English, History, Geography, Reading and Writing. They also insisted that both the headmaster and under-master be university graduates, and fixed their salaries at £200 and £150 a year respectively.

Despite the changes, the complaints continued. The quality of the headmasters varied. Some, it seems, had other interests at heart. When the Reverend William Fletcher retired in 1872 he put up for sale his cellar of over 800 bottles of port, sherry, claret, madeira and hock.[8]

By 1905 the school was providing an education to 27 boarders and 37 day boys. By 1936 the numbers had risen to about 300 and new buildings were constructed opposite the Victorian school. The inadequacies of its site in the centre of the town were finally recognized in the post-war years and as soon as funds were available a new school was built at Hillbutts, about a mile to the west of the town. Later educational reorganization has in turn led to the introduction of the comprehensive system and in 1974 a middle school was built in East Borough.

Coles hardware shop in the High Street in the 1920s. This is now the Priest's House Museum.

YOUNG GENTLEMEN
Are Boarded & Educated,
BY
MR. P. HAWKE,
WIMBORNE, DORSET,
ON THE FOLLOWING TERMS.

ENTRANCE, ONE GUINEA.

Board, and Instruction in the English Language,
Geography with the use of the Globes and Maps,
Land-Surveying, and the most useful parts of the
Mathematics, Book-keeping by Single and Double
Entry, Drawing, &c.

TWENTY GUINEAS PER ANNUM.

Writing and Arithmetic .... 2 Guineas.
Washing.......................... 2 Ditto.
The Classics...................... 2 Ditto.
Day Scholars..................... 4 Ditto.

The Health and Comfort of the Young Gentlemen,
as well as their Improvement in intellectual and moral Science, are objects to which the attention of
Mr. H. is constantly directed.

N. B. Bills are requested to be settled half-yearly, and
a quarter's Notice is desired previously to the removal of
a Pupil from School.

Wimborne, December 21st, 1820.

ABRAHAM, PRINTER, WIMBORNE.

A card advertising Mr P. Hawke's boarding school for 'Young Gentleman' in 1820.

The Grammar School was not the only school in the 19th century town. Apart from the National School (founded in King Street in 1843), several private schools opened their doors as Wimborne became increasingly middle-class. Amongst them was Peter Hawke's, which by 1815 offered tuition in English language, writing and arithmetic. Charles Bowle, formerly under-master at the Grammar School, opened a 'Gentleman's boarding school' in 1832 to provide a 'classical education' to the sons of the local gentry. By 1848 there were two 'Academies' for 'Young Ladies', one in West Borough and one in Church Street. Other schools briefly appeared, then vanished; and in 1875 the town possessed three 'Ladies' schools, two preparatory schools and a private tutor.[9]

On the day of Queen Victoria's Coronation in June 1838 the 190 inmates of the workhouse were treated to a 'Beef & plum pudding' dinner and each was given a pint of beer. It was an uncharacteristic gesture, for following the New Poor Law of 1834 conditions in the Wimborne workhouse had steadily worsened. The act had introduced the principle of 'less eligibility', which in plain language meant that conditions in the workhouse had to be worse than those of the most menial work outside it. The act had also made Wimborne (with Cranborne) the centre of a poor law union that embraced 24 parishes. The results were overcrowding, disease, and a regime that treated the poor as if they were criminals.

The main occupation of the inmates was the picking of oakum (the fibres from old ropes), and the accounts record the purchase of 'fine oakum' in a sale at Portsmouth Dockyard in 1837.[10] Each able-bodied person was obliged to pick 4 pounds a day, an amount that had increased to 6 pounds by 1870. The work was arduous, and not helped by the diet, which in 1841 saw the discontinuing of the beer allowance and an overall reduction to a breakfast of milk or meat broth, meat once a week and 6 pounds of bread a week.[11] Only the sick received special rations, for the commonest prescription for most ailments was the drinking of tea and the addition of gin or port to the diet.[12] The only vegetables eaten were potatoes, making scurvy and rickets common, and in 1849 a doctor was called in to advise on the wisdom of making other vegetables available.

A group of pupils from Standard 1 with their mistress outside the National School in King Street in about 1905. Smiles seem singularly lacking in this group of scholars!

The hustings in Wimborne Square during the 1910 election campaign. The Liberal candidate, Frederick Edward Guest (1875-1937), was successfully returned for the first time in a contest with Colonel Nicholson (Conservative). Guest remained M.P. for East Dorset until 1922.

Two years earlier there had been an outbreak of smallpox in the workhouse. It quickly spread, for most of the 190 inmates slept in an attic dormitory intended to sleep no more than 40. Other diseases were as common. In 1861 twenty-year-old Sophia Cross died of pulmonary tuberculosis, and another inmate fell victim to pneumonia. Two years later there was a death from consumption and a case of rickets so severe that the doctor described fifteen-year-old George Forward as 'a fit case for an orthopaedic hospital.'

Various attempts were made to improve conditions. A chaplain was appointed, and a schoolmistress was employed to teach the children — who in 1841 included two boys of three and four days old. But discipline remained harsh, and so strictly were the sexes segregated that after morning service the men and boys were locked in their ward before the women were allowed to leave the chapel. Christianity posed inevitable problems. In 1881 the Reverend Carr John Glyn was so concerned about the 'objectionable passages to be found in *Hymns Ancient and Modern*' that he offered to provide an expurgated version, which the inmates could then sing accompanied by the recently installed old organ from Corfe Mullen.[13]

By the end of the century life in the workhouse had improved considerably. The children were taken on outings, tobacco and cakes were given as gifts, special dinners were provided at Christmas and a nurse had begun working in the infirmary. In 1929 responsibility for the workhouse was handed over to Dorset County Council. With the advent of a Welfare State the principles that had instituted it were finally abandoned. In August 1958, after nearly two centuries in the town, it was demolished.

The 1884 bill-head of W.J. Beck, a 'Furnishings and General Ironmonger' in East Brook. Note the range of his goods and services.

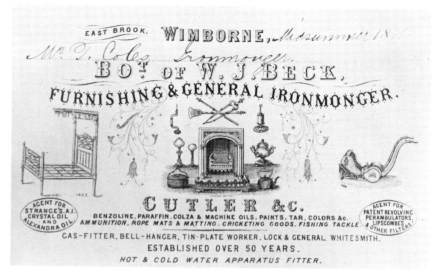

By the end of the 19th century Wimborne had acquired most of the benefits offered by the Industrial Revolution. In January 1837 the first shareholders in the Wimborne Minster Gas & Coal Co. met in the New Inn. Their acceptance of a tender for the construction of a gas works for £1,400 led to the placing of a token lamp standard opposite the inn. In the following year it was joined by a further twenty-seven posts, spread throughout the town. They were lit between March and September, burning from an hour after sunset to an hour before sunrise except for the five days round the full moon. The magistrates refusal to impose a rate for lighting made the company's history erratic, and in 1870 it was wound up and replaced by the Wimborne Minster Gas Company, a more successful and profitable venture which in 1935 became part of the Bournemouth Gas & Water Co.[14]

Until 1887 Wimborne's water came directly from the rivers or from easily polluted wells. But the formation of the Wimborne Minster Water Works Co. led to an artesian well being sunk at Walford and the laying of pipes through the streets. By 1910 its supplies had reached 17 million gallons a year, and four years later it was taken over by the Bournemouth Water

A new gasometer under construction alongside the railway embankment in Leigh Road in about 1910.

Company — which has since supplied the town, and whose impressive pumping station still stands on the north bank of the Allen west of the Crown and Anchor Inn.[15]

Electricity arrived in 1929 when the Bournemouth & Poole Electricity Supply Co connected the town to its Bourne Valley generators. It is now taken from the National Grid, and the pylons striding across the meadows near Roger Gillingham's almshouses and school at Pamphill span more than three centuries of parish improvement.

Perhaps the most significant 19th century improvement was the opening of the Victoria Hospital in 1887 to mark Queen Victoria's Golden Jubilee. The land was given on a 99 year lease by Sir John Hanham at an annual rent of 5s., providing it was used 'for the poor.' It initially had only thirty beds, and in its early years it was plagued by a lack of funds. In the 1930s it was extended; when it was simultaneously decided that admissions could be permitted from the surrounding countryside as well as just the town of Wimborne. By the time it was taken over by the National Health Service in 1947 no fewer than 591 patients had been treated and 136 major operations had been performed. It was an achievement of which Wimborne could be proud.

If Wimborne had to wait until the end of the century for its hospital, it could not make the same complaint about the railway. It arrived in June 1847, making Wimborne station the first to open in Dorset. One of its principal promoters was Charles Castleman of Allendale House, and it was

Wimborne postmen outside the East Street Post Office in about 1890.

East Street, decorated to commemorate Queen Victoria's Diamond Jubilee in 1897. Note the postman on his tricycle: letters were carried in the pannier beneath his seat.

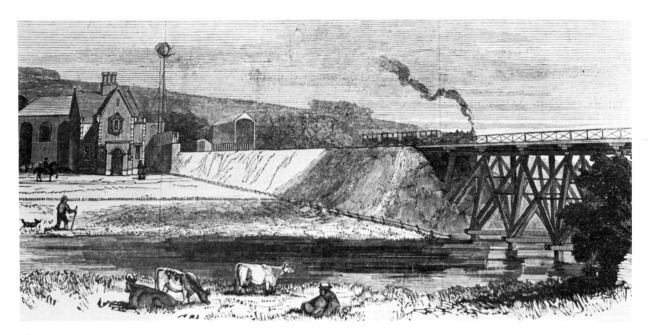

The Southampton and Dorchester Railway at Wimborne in 1847. Note the wooden trestle viaduct over the River Stour and the tall, distinctive signal on what was then a single-track line. Lord de Mauley of Canford, one of the original supporters of the railway, wanted the station to be built on the south side of the river for the convenience of his estate. Castleman's influence ensured that it was built in Wimborne.

Castleman who first realized the effect the opening of a railway between Southampton and Dorchester would have on the market towns of south-east Dorset. Despite the differences between the promoters over the route, Castleman was determined that it should pass through Wimborne. The circuitous sixty mile route (which led to it being nicknamed 'Castleman's Corkscrew') was finally agreed when the engineer, Captain W.S. Moorsom, presented his report to a committee meeting at the Crown Hotel in the Square in 1844.[16] As was often the case in the early years of the railways there was endless in-fighting amongst rival interests, but by June 1847 the Southampton and Dorchester Railway was ready to open. Some regretted its arrival, amongst them John Hanham who in a letter to his father from India feared its effects on the partridge shooting over the estate.

Few shared Hanham's doubts. The railway transformed the town. By linking Wimborne to London and reducing the time needed to get there from fourteen to under four hours it attracted new inhabitants. The trade directories reflect the wider choice of goods that could be bought in the shops. Its impact on farming was considerable. As well as opening new markets to the farmers themselves, agricultural merchants like James Sykes were soon advertising 'Artificial Manures, Nitrate of Soda, Potato Manure … and Oat Manures,' as well as 'Dissolved Bones and McDougall's Royal Patent Feeding Cakes for Lambs and Calves.'

Other railways soon followed the Southampton and Dorchester. The first stretch of the Dorset Central Railway, linking Blandford to Wimborne, was opened in 1860. Two years later it amalgamated with the Somerset Central Railway, making Wimborne the most important railway junction and depot in Dorset. Its glory was short-lived, for in 1884 a loop was constructed between Corfe Mullen and Broadstone which enabled trains to reach Poole without passing through Wimborne.[17]

The first to suffer from the opening of the railways were those who had invested in the turnpikes. The last of them, the Puddletown and Wimborne Trust, had only opened seven years before the arrival of the railway, and its route between Wimborne and Dorchester virtually duplicated that of the railway. By the date of its closure in 1876 its principal promoter, J.S.W. Sawbridge Erle Drax of Charborough Park, had lost an estimated £48,000.[18] When the road between Wimborne and Blandford closed in 1883, the age of the Wimborne turnpikes was over.

The carriers and coach services were also affected by the railways. But they were more adaptable, changing their time-tables to coincide with the arrival and departure of the trains. The carriers survived until the charabanc made them redundant, acting as the traditional ferry for both goods and people between the town and outlying villages.

In 1881 Thomas Hardy and his wife moved into one of Wimborne's new villas, Lanherne (No. 16), in Avenue Road. They stayed two years, both of which Hardy enjoyed, for he found pleasure and stimulation in Wimborne society. He also wrote one of his few humorous poems whilst living in the town, *The Levelled Churchyard*, in response to the recent levelling of the minster churchyard and the redistribution of the tombstones. Two of its verses read:

The High Street and railed minster graveyard in the mid-19th century.

> Where we are huddled none can trace,
> And if our names remain,
> They have some path or porch or place
> Where we have never lain!

> Here's not a modest maiden elf
> But dreads the final Trumpet,
> Lest half of her should rise herself,
> And half some sturdy strumpet!

The levelling of the churchyard, and indeed Hardy's presence, were indications that Wimborne's character was changing. The march of the red brick villas into the countryside had begun. The developing suburbs of Rowlands and Colehill provided villas 'for retired officers on half pay, artists, clergymen and the professional classes generally'.[19] From their windows, they could look down on the gypsies in the fields off Leigh Road and the slate roofs of the terraced houses that had been built in a group of newly

Elliot Brothers 'Royal Blue' coach standing outside Curtis's auctioneers in Bournemouth before its journey to Canford and Wimborne.

Suburban development in the late 19th century, Avenue Road. The houses stood in their own gardens and looked out over the tree-lined avenues so much in vogue during the period of Wimborne's first expansion.

Tickets issued for dinner and grog with the Odd Fellows in June 1863, and a subscription ticket for the use of the White Hart skittle ground.

laid out roads (Grove, St Catherine's, Ethelbert, Crescent and New Borough) between Poole Road and the railway station. In 1876 the town's markets and fairs were abolished. The cattle market was moved to a field on the outskirts of town and the weekly corn market was relegated to the Corn Exchange.

By the middle of the 19th century the minster churchyard was too small for its purpose and in 1856 a new cemetery was laid out between Stone Lane and St Margaret's Hill. One of the first people to be buried in it was John Hanham. After serving in the 1st Sikh War, he had returned to England and was murdered by a private. His younger brother Thomas was one of the founding fathers of cremation, and, after building a crematorium at Manston House on the banks of the Stour, he became known to other members of the family as 'Stoker' Hanham.

As the town changed, so too did the larger houses that surrounded it. Most dramatic of the changes were those at Kingston Lacy. The alterations made by the architect Sir Charles Barry included the complete refacing of the house in Chilmark stone (now a major problem for the National Trust who in 1982 are having to replace all the iron clasps used during the refacing with stainless steel). As well as adding four large chimneys at each corner and dormer windows, the interior was partially gutted and completely redecorated. By the middle of the 19th century the outlawed (for homosexuality) eccentric, William John Bankes, had begun sending a collection of antiquities back to the house to join the Egyptian obelisk which had been set up in the park in 1827. On his death in Venice in 1855 special parliamentary permission was obtained for his body to be brought back to England so that he could be buried with his ancestors in the Bankes' vault in the minster church.

Despite the various changes to the town and surrounding countryside, 19th century Wimborne had not forgotten how to enjoy itself. When a West Street baker was sent to Dorchester Prison for drunkenness, the crowds gathered at the station to welcome him home on the day of his release

Kingston Lacy from the north-east, showing Sir Charles Barry's mid 19th century alterations.

carried him in triumph through the streets. A Captain Boyton enjoyed his retirement floating down the Allen 'enveloped in his new dress of rubber from head to foot, rowing himself swiftly along by means of a paddle.' Men like John Shittler and Henry Small of Bradford and Barford Farms' were keen agriculturalists, and early members of the Royal Agricultural Society. On public holidays the population took boats on the Stour or embarked in carriers' carts for Bournemouth's beaches or the Larmer Tree Grounds and picnicked on eels, whitebait, haunches of mutton, tarts and custard.

Canford Bridge in about 1920. The bridge spans the Stour and links Wimborne to Poole. A tablet on it reads: 'This Bridge finished in the year 1813 by John Dyson, Engineer, Jesse Bushrod, Mason.

The scene in East Street following the fire of 1905. On the right is the gutted remains of Hawker's drapery and outfitter's shop: note its steel girders. The town's horse-drawn steam-pump fire engine stands beneath the gas lamp outside the Post Office.

East Street in the 1920s. Fosters outfitter's occupies Hawker's rebuilt shop. A gas mantle has replaced the fish-tail burner seen in the photograph taken after the 1905 fire.

On a hot August day in 1864 fire broke out in the thatched house of a laundress in East Borough. In an hour twelve houses and a pub had been destroyed. The fire engine had arrived promptly, but at first could not be made to work.[20] The result was the formation of a Volunteer Fire Brigade and the replacement of the original engine with a new appliance that required sixteen men to operate the pumps. In 1900 it too was made redundant, and a steam-powered pump with a boiler at the rear was acquired in its place. Five years later there was a second fire in the town. It began in a draper's shop in East Street, and at least one person escaped from the flames by jumping into the mill stream.

The modernization of the town's fire-fighting equipment was typical of 19th century civic progress. By 1853 the 'blind house' had been used for the last time: with tragic results, for the two vagrants locked inside it choked to death after setting fire to the straw. Two years later the County Constabulary was established and Wimborne was provided with a superintendent, sergeant and ten constables in place of the last parish constables, William Duffall and James Galpin, whose tall black hats and blue coats with brass buttons made them a familiar sight in the town.

Wimborne's last links with its medieval past were gradually disappearing. The livestock had vanished from the streets. Railings surrounded the churchyard. In 1846 the Court of the Royal Peculiar was abolished, having shed its powers to other bodies. Nearly fifty years later, in 1894, the Wimborne Urban District Council was established. The century had turned full circle, and we shall leave it with a story which is more typical of its start than its close. In 1829 the Corporation gave a dinner for the Bishop of Bristol. By the time the twenty-five people who attended the dinner rose from the table they had consumed 13 bottles of port, 13 bottles of sherry, 10 bowls of punch and a large quantity of beer, porter and cider. The result was a public outcry, but such excesses evoke a world that was soon to be extinct.

William Duffall, one of Wimborne's last two parish constables. The original portrait hangs in The Priest's House Museum.

Wimborne Volunteer Fire Brigade with their Merryweather fire engine in 1932. The fire station was then in East Borough. Henry Cowdry was chief officer, Robert Cribb his second in command.

Two views of the disused, derelict and overgrown station as it is today. The site is soon to be developed.

The pedestrian shopping precinct built between the Mill Stream and Allen (1979-81). The central tower of the minster is visible in the background.

The impact of the 20th century on Wimborne life is still hard to gauge. Local government re-organization in 1974 made the town the centre of the Wimborne District Council. The railway was closed in 1964, a victim of the Beeching Plan, but a line was kept open to serve the army oil stores at West Moors. It finally closed in the 1970s, and both the bridge over Leigh Road and the steel viaduct over the Stour have been demolished. After remaining derelict for some years, the station site is now being developed. In September 1981 the town finally acquired the by-pass (A31) it so desperately needed to reduce the traffic through its centre. The Cornmarket has recently been closed to cars and laid out as an attractive open space. The construction of the Allendale Community Centre has provided a focus for Wimborne's cultural and social life. Both the fire and police services have been given new premises in Hanham Road, and opposite them stand a headquarters for the ambulance service and a modern medical clinic. The influx of light manufacturing and marketing industries into Knobcrook and the Leigh Estate on the north bank of the Stour has helped the town to maintain its prosperity.

But the story is not one of complete success. Problems such as parking still pose a threat to Wimborne's character. In the 1950s, many buildings of historic or architectural importance were demolished: amongst which were a group of cottages near the minster in King Street and Lady Gertrude's Almshouses in Dean's Court Lane.

Some of the demolition has been unavoidable, for Wimborne has grown substantially throughout the 20th century. Many of the villas in the Leigh area have been turned into flats or replaced by newer houses. Development took place along Victoria Road and to the north of Walford Bridge in the years between the wars. Colehill was also further developed between the wars, but the main expansion has taken place more recently.

Wimborne's centre has not been spared the need to make full use of all the available space. Its shops still retain a hint of their market town character, but the arrival of the larger chain stores has brought change to the heart of the town. A shopping mall and a well-stocked country branch library have been constructed alongside the Allen. Church House was built in 1905 on the site of the old Angel Inn. After a long period of redundancy, the Crown Inn in the Square has been demolished and replaced by offices, shops and town houses.

Men of Wimborne parade outside the railway station in the late summer of 1914 – volunteers for Kitchener's army. Note the now demolished Griffin Hotel to the right.

PRECAUTIONARY MEASURES
against
ATTACKS BY
AIRCRAFT.
DEFENCE OF THE REALM ACT. 1914.
WIMBORNE MINSTER.
PUBLIC WARNING.

A poster issued in 1914 advising Wimburnians of the precautions they should take if attacked from the air.

Nor was Wimborne spared the realities of two World Wars. Between 1914 and 1918 names like Amiens, Bapaume, Arras and Cambrai became household words in the town. Out of a population in Wimborne, Colehill, Holt and Pamphill of about 6,500, 571 saw service overseas, and the names of the 164 who never returned are remembered by a tablet in the north transept of the minster that lists their names.

In 1939 war broke out again. A second tablet in the south transept of the minster records the names of the 32 Wimburnians who died between 1939 and 1945. Following Dunkirk the Home Guard was established, and for the next four years the town and surrounding parishes saw members of the Sixth Battalion The Dorset (Home Guard) Regiment taking up their posts whenever an air raid threatened. But the town escaped lightly. The main damage was caused by incendaries, but after a total of forty-seven raids only two people had been killed and twenty-two injured. Kingston Lacy became an American field hospital, and Wimborne Fire Brigade travelled as far afield as Bristol, Plymouth and Southampton to help fight the fires that followed the worst of the raids.[21]

Wimborne's Auxiliary Fire Service leading a procession through the town during 'Warships Savings Week' in 1941.

Wimborne Home Guard, 6th Battalion Signals. Note the carrier pigeons in their boxes.

The Bournemouth registered 'Milk, Passenger and Goods Service' bus. The bus operated a twice-daily service and stopped at Wimborne on both occasions.

Wimborne's first car, owned by Mr Tilley and photographed here in about 1900.

F.W. Barratt & Co, East Street 'Motor Engineers', in about 1912. Barratt's began life as an ironmonger's.

The First World War had proved the value of motor transport, and in 1919 the first bus service between Wimborne and Bournemouth was established. Within the next two years both Blandford and Shaftesbury had been brought closer to the town by the early buses of the Hants & Dorset Motor Co. The motor car had made its first appearance in Wimborne by the turn of the century, and in 1902 the young Wimborne doctor, Kaye le Fleming, sold his pony and trap and bought a Benz car to improve his rural practice. Some did not approve: on a visit to Crichel House Kaye le Fleming was informed by the butler that Lord Alington wanted the Benz removed from the park. But Lord Alington's dislike of the car did not last, for in 1906 the first rally of the Dorset Automobile Club was held in Crichel Park.[22] By 1912 Wimborne had its own garage, and a trade directory of 1935 lists seven garages and motor engineers.

The car has transformed Wimborne Minster, and the blessings it has brought have been mixed. But the growth of tourism it helped inspire has made the conservation of Wimborne's spiritual and architectural heritage increasingly important. Not for the first time in its history, Wimborne's site has proved an advantage. When Henry Ralph Bankes died in August 1981 he left to the National Trust the biggest gift in its history — the Kingston Lacy estate. As well as the house and park, the National Trust have acquired Pamphill, Cowgrove, a large area of Colehill, part of Wimborne, God Blessing Green, Holt Wood and Holt Forest and Heath. The house contains one of the finest collections of paintings in the country, and once it is opened it will add to Wimborne's visitors — just as the minster, model village and gardens at Dean's Court have done already.

When I first began researching into Wimborne's history I had no idea as to how enjoyable the journey into its past would become. Its story has always been absorbing, and often surprising. The placid respectability of its present conceals a rich heritage. Time has seen it flourish, and the English country town that is Wimborne Minster today can face its future with optimism and pride.

Appendix

TABLE I

LAY SUBSIDY ROLL, 1327

Tithing	No. of names	6d.	7d.	8d.	9d.	12d.	18d.	20d.	2.	3s.	3s.4d.	5s.	Total tax
						Number of individual tax assessments							
Wimborne Minster	71	47	0	2	2	12	4	0	3	0	0	1	£2. 15s. 4d.
Barnsley Farm	24	15	1	1	3	3	0	0	0	1	0	0	17s. 0d.
Kingston Lacy*	117	–	–	–	–	–	–	–	–	–	–	–	£5. 10s. 11d.
Leigh	81	43	0	1	3	23	3	1	5	2	0	0	£3. 9s. 7d.
Petersham (Holt)	19	6	0	0	0	7	1	0	?	0	3	0	£1. 5s. 6d.

LAY SUBSIDY ROLL, 1332

Tithing	No. of names	8d.	10d.	12d.	16d.	20d.	22d.	2s.	3s.	3/4	4s.	6/8	20s.	Total tax
					Number of individual tax assessments									
Wimborne Minster	73	52	0	12	4	0	0	4	1	0	0	0	0	£3. 3s. 0d.
Barnsley Farm	25	10	2	3	2	0	1	5	1	0	1	0	0	£1. 12s. 10d.
Kingston Lacy	114	50	20	20	6	2	1	4	5	0	4	1	1	£7. 8s. 10d.
Leigh	87	55	1	12	9	1	0	3	3	0	3	0	0	£4. 10s. 2d.
Petersham (Holt)	19	10	0	5	3	0	0	0	0	1	0	0	0	19s. 0d.

*Damage to the roll means that many of the individual assessments are lost. Fortunately the total number of tax payers and the total sum collected are preserved.

TABLE II
Lay Subsidy Rolls, Estimated Population Figures

Year	Tithing	No. of taxpayers	Total population (est.)
1327	Wimborne Minster	71	320
	Barnsley Farm	24	108
	Kingston Lacy	117	527
	Leigh	81	364
	Petersham	19	86
	Total for parish	312	1,405
1332	Wimborne Minster	73	328
	Barnsley Farm	25	113
	Kingston Lacy	114	511
	Leigh	87	392
	Petersham	19	86
	Total for parish	318	1,430

TABLE III

Wimborne Parish: Hearth Tax Analysis 1662-4

Number of hearths per house*

Tithing	1	2	3	4	5	6	7	8	9	10	11	12	13	24	Paupers
Abbot Street	4	7	5	3	0	0	0	0	0	0	0	0	0	0	1
Barnsley	9	1	4	1	1	1	0	1	0	0	0	0	0	0	0
Cowgrove	20	9	6	5	2	0	0	0	1	0	0	0	0	0	1
Leigh	24	17	5	2	4	0	0	0	0	0	0	0	0	0	7
Petersham	0	3	6	1	0	0	7	0	0	0	0	0	0	0	0
Stone	18	16	6	4	1	1	0	1	0	0	0	0	1	0	1
Thornhill	28	7	3	2	0	1	0	0	0	0	0	0	0	0	8
Wimborne Borough	11	5	6	4	4	1	0	0	0	0	0	0	0	0	3
Wimborne Town	42	44	14	8	8	5	3	3	1	2	1	1	0	1	28
Total hearths	156	109	55	30	20	9	10	5	2	2	1	1	1	1	49

* The numbers are as originally recorded: alterations such as 'stopt' or 'downe' have been ignored in these calculations as such modifications indicated a later reaction to the original arrangement of hearths. Note: a very few entries are not quite clear so there could be a small percentage error in the figures. These, however, are so few that they would be most unlikely to alter the overall trend.

TABLE IV

Wimborne (Whole Parish) Poor Rate Income and Expenditure
for Selected Groups of Years in the 18th Century

Year	Income	No. of Rates	Expenditure	Balance
	£ s. d.		£ s. d.	£ s. d.
1700-01	364. 13. 9¼	5	332. 19. 3¼	+ 31. 14. 6
1701-02	326. 8. 9	5	334. 9. 11½	− 8. 1. 2½
1702-03	329. 11. 5½	5	320. 12. 10	+ 8. 18. 7½
1703-04	259. 15. 0	4	249. 17. 3	+ 9. 17. 9
1704-05	259. 8. 8	4	243. 16. 6½	+ 15. 12. 1½
1705-06	262. 15. 4½	4	259. 4. 2	+ 3. 11. 2½
1706-07	257. 15. 0	4	255. 14. 0	+ 2. 1. 0
1707-08	288. 3. 9	4	282. 12. 10	+ 5. 10. 11
1708-09	323. 17. 1	5	322. 12. 7	+ 1. 4. 6
1709-10	386. 5. 6	6	389. 17. 7	− 3. 12. 1
1710-11	450. 2. 7	7	459. 0. 1	− 8. 17. 6
1723-24	311. 9. 2	5	308. 18. 2	+ 2. 11. 0
1724-25	373. 2. 6	6	367. 2. 4	+ 6. 0. 2
1725-26	375. 5. 9	6	327. 9. 0	+ 47. 16. 9
1726-27	388. 6. 8	6	379. 4. 8	+ 9. 2. 0
1727-28	433. 8. 4	6½	413. 15. 1	+ 19. 13. 3
1760-61*	882. 12. 3	12	842. 3. 8¼	+ 40. 8. 6¾
1761-62*	709. 8. 2¼	12	717. 9. 7¼	+ 10. 8. 7¼
1762-63	709. 8. 1¼	12	693. 9. 0	+ 15. 19. 1¼
1763-64	671. 7. 11	11	653. 7. 1¾	+ 19. 0. 9¼
1764-65	720. 14. 7¾	12	749. 6. 0	− 28. 11. 4¼
1765-66	794. 4. 10	14	853. 3. 6½	− 58. 18. 8½
1766-77	913. 9. 8	16	994. 14. 4¾	− 81. 4. 8¾
1767-68	929. 14. 5¼	16	1,012. 5. 11½	− 82. 11. 6¼
1768-69	916. 15. 0¼	16	912. 7. 10¾	+ 4. 7. 1½
1769-70	921. 10. 10	16	897. 18. 1¾	+ 23. 12. 8¼

Year	Income	No. of Rates	Expenditure	Balance
1796-97	1,660. 18. 10	29	1,660. 1. 10	+ 17. 0
1797-98	1,424. 13. 5	25	1,398. 6. 2	+26. 7. 3
1798-99	1,466. 1. 9½	25	1,387. 10. 11½	+78. 10. 10
1799-1800	1,866. 5. 0	30	1,837. 6. 0	+28. 19. 0
1800-01	4,106. 16. 11½	71	4,062. 9. 6	+44. 7. 5½

Note: As an example of true rating income the years marked with an asterisk (*) each brought in about £650 on 12 rates. The higher sum is made up from rents, moneys brought forward and charitable income directed towards the poor rate.

Notes

Abbreviations

Dorset Procs., The Proceedings of the D.N.H. & A.S.
S.D.N.Q., Somerset & Dorset Notes & Queries
VCH, Victoria County History
R.C.H.M., Royal Commission on Historical Monuments
D.C.R.O., Dorset County Record Office

CHAPTER 1

1. Barker, K., 'Early Ecclesiastical Settlement in Dorset', *Dorset Procs., 102* (1980), 109-111.
2. *The Anglo-Saxon Chronicle*, edit. G.N. Garmonsway (2nd. edit. 1954), 42.
3. Taylor, C.C., 'Wimborne Minster', *Dorset Procs., 89* (1967), 170: also Penn, K.J., *Historic Towns of Dorset* (1980), 121 and 125.
4. For a convenient up-to-date history of the Burghal Hidage see: Hinton, D.A., *Alfred's Kingdom* (1977), 30-41.
5. Quoted by Calthrop, M.M.C., 'Religious Houses: Wimborne Minster' *VCH Dorset II* (1908), 111.
6. Clegg, A.L., *A History of Wimborne Minster & District (1960), 26.*
7. *Farrar, R.A.H., 'Some Roman Tessarae under the Nave of Wimborne Minster', Dorset Procs., 84* (1962), 106.
8. R.C.H.M. *Dorset, V, East* (1976), 80.
9. Calthrop, *op. cit.*, 109 and other sources.
10. Clegg., *op. cit.*, 27.
11. Mills, A.D., *The Place-Names of Dorset, Part II* (1980), 163 and for Wimborne Minster 183-193; Colehill 136-140; Holt 150-158.

CHAPTER 2

1. Darby, H.C., 'Dorset', Darby, H.C. & Flinn, R.W., *The Domesday Geography of South-West England* (1979 reprint), 117.
2. A hide was an area of land that has never been satisfactorily explained. It was a unit of tax assessment originally constituted to support one family. Some authorities have estimated the Dorset hide at 120 acres.
3. The source for all Domesday entries and translations is: Williams, A., 'Text of the Dorset Domesday', *VCH Dorset III* (1968), edit. R.B. Pugh.
4. ibid., Nos. 6 and 90.
5. ibid., Nos. 73 and 100.

CHAPTER 3

1. Fletcher, J.M.J., 'A Dorset Royal Peculiar', *Dorset Procs., 38* (1917), 93-5.
2. Calthrop, *op. cit.*, 110.
3. Calthrop, *op. cit.*, and Hutchins, J., *Hist. of Dorset, III* (3rd. edit. 1868, edit. Shipp & Hodson), 184.
4. *The Registers of Roger Martival, Bishop of Salisbury, 1315-30, III* (1965), edit. S. Reynolds, Nos. 157 and 169.
5. R.C.H.M. *Dorset V, op. cit.*, 80-1.
6. Calthrop, *op. cit.*, 109.
7. Housden, J.A.J., 'Canons of Wimborne', *S.D.N.Q., X,* 109.
8. *Cal. of Papal Registers, Petitions I, 1342-1419*, No. 1335 (Apr. 1335), incompletely quoted by Housden.
9. *Cal. of Inquisitions Miscellaneous, 1307-49*, No. 1614.
10. Calthrop, *op. cit.*, 110: Clegg, *op. cit.*, 36-7.
11. *Itinerary of King Edward the First throughout his Reign, A.D. 1272-1307* (1900) edt. H. Gough.
12. *Liberate Rolls IV, 1251-60*, 88 (21/11/1252).
13. Field, N.H ., 'The Leaze, Wimborne', *Dorset Procs., 94* (1972), 59.
14. *ibid.*
15. Taylor, *op. cit.*, 168-170.
16. Coram Rege Roll, 29/m.. 11d., quoted in *ibid.*, 170.
17. Clegg., *op. cit.*, 183.
18. Ex-info. Mr. David Smith reporting Miss P.M. Cunnington, R.I.B.A., who made the plausible conjecture recorded here, May 1980.
19. Sumner, H., *Local Papers* (1931), 39.
20. Quoted in Clegg, *op. cit.*, 257.
21. *ibid.*, 192
22. Field, *op. cit.*, 60 and n. 3.

CHAPTER 4

1. Rumble, Subsidy Roll, *op. cit.*, 123.
2. Mills, Subsidy Roll, *op. cit.*, 101.
3. Fripp, M.C., & Wragge, P., 'Social and Economic History' *VCH Dorset, II*, 240.
4. Fletcher, J.M.J., 'The Churchwardens' Accounts of Wimborne Minster', *S.D.N .Q. XXII*, 103 – 104.
5. Fleming, E.K. le, 'Wimborne Minster Churchwardens' Accounts', *S.O.N.Q. XV*, 179.
6. D.C.R.O. Kingston Lacy Inclosure Act 1786 and map.
7. Fry, E.A., 'Court Roll of Kingston Lacy, Dorset', *S.D.N.Q. VIII*, 303.
8. Fripp & Wragge, *op. cit.*, 240.
9. *ibid.*
10. *The Brokerage Book of Southampton 1443-4, I*, edited by O. Coleman (1961), 24.
11. Fleming, *op. cit.*, 103-4.
12. Hutchins, *op. cit.*, 257.
13. Names from the Subsidy Rolls, *op. cit.*; see also Reaney, P.H., *A Dictionary of British Surnames* (2nd edit. 1976).
14. All foregoing notes taken from the three published sets of churchwardens' accounts.
15. Fripp & Wragge, *op. cit.*, 240.
16. Hutchins, *op. cit.*, 245; Warren, P.J.K., 'The Story of Holt Church and Holt Forest, Wimborne', *Dorset Procs. 88* (1966), 189.
17. Clegg, *op. cit.*, 133.
18. Calthrop, *op. cit.*, 106., Hutchins, *op. cit.*, 247., Fletcher, W.J., 'St Margaret's Hospital, Wimborne Minster', *Dorset Procs. 17* (1896), 109-10., Clegg, *op. cit.*, 133., *Report of the Charity Commissioners, Dorset*, 61.

19. Fletcher, W.J., *op. cit.*, 111., Clegg, *op. cit.*, 133 (Clegg has misread day of month for regnal year).
20. Fletcher, W.J., *op. cit.*, 110.
21. Hutchins, *op. cit.*, 248-9.
22. Harl. Mss. 6963, fol. 56, quoted in Clegg, *op. cit.*, 143; Calthrop, *op. cit.*, 110 n. 34.
23. For the story of the tower see Hutchins, *op. cit.*, 206.
24. Tribe, T. & Whatmoor, P., *Dorset Clocks and Clockmakers (1981)* – a valuable account to which I am indebted.
25. *ibid.*, 153 – 5.
26. Fleming, *op. cit.*
27. Hutchins *op. cit.*, 226., Warren, *op. cit.*, 189.
28. Warren, *ibid.*, 188-9.
29. Quoted by Tipping, H.A., 'Margaret Beaufort' entry, *Dictionary of National Biography*.
30. Tipping, H.A., 'John Beaufort' entry, *ibid.*
31. Hutchins, *op. cit.*, 191., Calthrop, *op. cit.*, 111.

CHAPTER 5

1. Chantry Cert. 16, No. 111 quoted in Calthrop, *op. cit.*
2. *ibid.*
3. Hutchins, *op. cit.*, 261.
4. *ibid.*
5. *ibid.*, 192.
6. *Report of the Charity Comm., op. cit.*, 53.
7. This and much subsequent information on the Hanham family from Hanham, D.C., 'The Hanhams of Wimborne Minster', *S.D.N.Q. XXXI, part 311 (1980)*, 27 – 31.
8. *ibid.*, part 312, 68.
9. Bankes, V., *A Dorset Heritage* (1953), 144; see also R.C.H.M. *Dorset V*, 46.
10. Hutchins, *op. cit.*, 228.
11. Information from: Stoate, T.L., *Dorset Tudor Muster Rolls* (1978), 98ff.
12. For discussion of 17th century house types see: R.C.H.M. *Dorset II South-east Part 1*, lx-ixiv., also Machin, R., *Probate Inventories & Manorial Excepts of Chetnole, Leigh and Yetminster* where buildings are related to inventories.
13. All Hearth Tax information derived from: Meekings, C.A.F., *the Dorset Hearth Tax 1662 – 64* (1951), 25-8.
14. Observations and drawings by Jude James, 1977.
15. DCRO. P204/CP2, 12.
16. *Ibid.*, 2.
17. Hutchins, *op. cit.*, 261.
18. DCRO. P204/CP1, 114.
19. Background to the Royal Peculiar: Fletcher, J.M.J., 'A Dorset Royal Peculiar', *Dorset Procs. 38* (1917), 93-111.
20. DCRO. P204/CP30, 131.
21. *Ibid.*, 9-18.
22. *Ibid.*, 31-2.
23. *Ibid.*, 33. For discussion of sexual morality see: Quaife, G.R., *Wanton Wenches and Wayward Wives* (1979), 91 – 3. It is a valuable study of 17th century conditions.
24. DCRO. P204/CP32, Presentments, 47.
25. *Ibid.*, 110.
26. *Ibid.*, 145.
27. *Ibid.*, 36 (15/1/1598).
28. Historical Mss. Commission, *Salisbury, Vol. 17*, 591 (114. 5-6).
29. DCRO. P204/CP31 and CP32.
30. DCRO. P204/CP32, Presentments, 99., see also Densham, W. & Ogle, J., *The Story of the Congregational Churches of Dorset* (1899), 385 – 6.
31. *Ibid.*, 387 – 9 (note date error p. 387).

32. DCRO. P204/CP30, 54 also CP32, 54.
33. DCRO. P204/CP32, Presentments, 94.
34. DCRO. P204/CP30, 128 (21/11/1638).
35. *Ibid.*, 116 (18/12/1638).
36. Story of shalloon factory from Densham & Ogle, *op. cit.*, 388.
37. This and all following information on charities from: *Report of the Charity Commissioners, Dorset, 53-73*: Hutchins, *op. cit.*, 247-252 and Clegg, *op. cit.*, 133 – 9 (note Clegg misnames Lyne as Lyme).
38. Hutchins, *op. cit.*, 260,262.
39. *Ibid.*, 263.
40. Quoted in *ibid.*, 199.
41. DCRO. P204/CP32, Presentments, 104. For list of repairs see Hutchins, *op. cit.*, 256-265.
42. *Ibid.*

CHAPTER 6

1. Hutchins, *op. cit.*, 265.
2. DCRO. P204/OV1.
3. *Ibid.*
4. *Ibid.*
5. DCRO. P204/OV4.
6. DCRO. P204/OV100.
7. DCRO. P204/OV4 (1/8/1769).
8. DCRO. P204/OV2.
9. DCRO. P204/OV91
10. DCRO. P204/VE1 (6/5/1750).
11. DCRO. P204/VE1 (26/4/1784).
12. *Ibid.*, (23/9/1800).
13. *Ibid.*, (17/4/1769).
14. DCRO. P204/VE2 (3/8/1818).
15. All the following examples are taken from the Hanham Manorial Court Books preserved at Dean's Court.
16. Information on turnpike roads is taken from parliamentry acts, minute books and accounts in the DCRO.
17. Fleming, E.K. le., 'The Records of the Turnpike Trustees of the Poole, Wimborne and Cranborne Trust', *Dorset Procs., 48 1(1927)*, 64.
18. DCRO. Dorset Quarter Sessions.
19. DCRO. P204/OV4 (3/8/1762).
20. DCRO. P204/VE1 (23/8/1761).
21. DCRO. P204/OV4 (3/8/1762 and 5/9/1762).
22. Details of traders abstracted from DCRO, VE and OV volumes.
23. *British Universal Directory* 1792, 763.
24. Symonds, H., 'West Country Bankers', *Dorset Procs. 68* (1927), 22.
25. Young, D.S., *The Story of Bournemouth* (1970 reprint), 22 – 3: Clegg, *op. cit.*, 186-7.
26. Building details largely from R.C.H.M. Dorset, *op. cit.*
27. British Direct., *op. cit.*, 766.
28. Bankes details from Bankes, V., *op. cit.*
29. DCRO. P204/CP30, 108.
30. DCRO. Kingston Lacy Inclosure Act.
31. *Dorchester and Sherborne Journal*, 23/12/1796, p.3, col. 4.
32. Gourlay, A.B., *A History of Sherborne School* (1971), 152n.
33. Farm details calculated from the Tithe Apportionment 1847 (DCRO) and family details from 1851 census (P.R.O., H.O. 107/1854).
34. *Ibid.*
35. *Dorset County Chronicle*, 5/10/1854, p.4, col. 4.
36. P.R.O. H.O.44/22.
37. Okeden, W.H.P., 'The Agricultural Riots in Dorset in 1830', *Dorset Procs. 52* (1930), 88-9: Clegg, *op. cit.*, 179.

CHAPTER 7

1. R.C.H.M., Dorset V, *op. cit.*, 85.
2. Hutchins, *op. cit.*, 252.
3. Information mainly from Matthews, B., *The Organ & Organists of Wimborne Minster 1408-1972* (c.1972).
4. Information on churches from *Kelly's Directories*, 1920, 1931 and 1935.
5. Densham & Ogle, *op. cit.*, 389.
6. *Ibid.*, 392.
7 Habgood, F.E. and Moore, A.O., *Wimborne Circuit of the Methodist Church 1850 – 1950* (1950).
8. Wyatt, D.G., 'Schooling in 19th Century Wimborne', *Wimborne in the Nineteenth Century*, edited by J. James (1978), 16.
9. Most information on schools from Wyatt, *ibid.*, 14-20.
10. Popham, D., 'Wimborne in 1837', *Dorset Magazine 33* (1974), 43.
11. Priest's House Museum, File Y/A.
12. DCRO. P204/OV86, Medical Relief Book.
13. Priest's Ho. Mus. File Y/A.
14. Gas work's history from Clegg, *opl cit.*, 154-5: Popham, *op. cit.*, 47.
15. Clegg, *op. cit.*, 153-4.
16. Southampton and Dorchester railway history from: Cox, J.C., *Castleman's Corkscrew* (1975).
17. Railway information from Lucking, J.H., *Railways of Dorset* (1968) and Atthill. R., *the Somerset and Dorset Railway* (1967).
18. *S.D.N.Q.* 17 (1923), 52.
19. Score, H.B., *Rambles in and around Wimborne Minster* (1921), 10.
20. Dorset County Chronicle, 18/8/1864, p.66, col. 4.
21. Clegg, *op. cit.*, 197-8.
22. Fleming, C. le., 'Doctor Before the Health Service – Sir Kaye le Fleming.' *Dorset Magazine* 43 (1975), 44 and Burnett D., *A Dorset Camera 1855-1914* (1974), illus. 132.

Select Bibliography

Atthill, R. *The Somerset & Dorset Railway* (Newton Abbot 1967)

Bankes, V. *A Dorset Heritage* (1953)

Clegg, A.L. *A History of Wimborne Minster & District* (Bournemouth 1960)

Cox, J.G. *Castleman's Corkscrew* (Southampton 1975)

Densham, W. & Ogle, J. *The Story of the Congregational Churches in Dorset* (Bournemouth 1899)

Douch, R. *A Handbook of Local History, Dorset* (Bristol 1962)

Good, R. *The Old Roads of Dorset* (Bournemouth 1966)

Hutchins, J. *The History and Antiquities of the County of Dorset, III* (3rd edition by W. Shipp & J.W. Hodson 1968, facsimile reprint 1973)

Loyd R. *Dorset Elizabethans* (1967)

Lucking, J.H. *Railways of Dorset* (Dorchester 1968)

Matthews, B. *The Organs and Organists of Wimborne Minster 1408 – 1972* (Wimborne n.d. *circa* 1972)

Mayo, C. *A History of Wimborne Minster* (1860)

Meekings, C.A.F. *Dorset Hearth Tax Assessments 1662 – 4* (Dorchester 1951)

Mills, A.D. *The Dorset Lay Subsidy Roll of 1332* (Dorchester 1971)

Mills, A.D. *The Place-Names of Dorset, Part II* (1980)

Penn, K.J. *Historic Towns in Dorset* (Dorchester 1980)

Perkins, T.L. *Wimborne Minster and Christchurch Priory* (1899)

Rumble, A.R. *The Dorset Lay Subsidy Roll of 1327* (Dorchester 1980)

Score, H.B. *Rambles in and around Wimborne Minster* by a 'Dorset Gentleman' (collection of newspaper cuttings, 1921-2)

Smith, H.P. *The History of the Borough and County of the Town of Poole, II* (Poole 1951)

Stoate, T.L. *Dorset Tudor Muster Rolls* (Bristol 1978)

Stoate, T.L. *Dorset Tudor Subsidies 1523-93* (Bristol 1982)

Taylor, C. *Dorset, The Making of the English Landscape* (1970)

Thomas, D. St J. *A Regional History of the Railways of Great Britain, I, The West Country* (Newton Abbot 1966)

Tribe, T. & Whatmoor, P. *Dorset Clocks and Clockmakers* (Oswestry 1981)

The Anglo-Saxon Chronicle edited by G.N. Garmonsway (1954)

The Dictionary of National Biography (Oxford 1975)

R.C.H.M. *Dorset, V, East* (1975)

The Victoria County History of Dorset, II (1908), edited by W. Page.

The Victoria County History of Dorset, III (1968), edited by R.B. Pugh.

Wimborne in the Nineteenth Century (Southampton 1978), edited by J. James.

Proceedings of the Dorset Natural History and Antiquarian (later *Archaeological*) *Society.Somerset and Dorset Notes and Queries*

Dorset Trade Directories (various 1792 – 1935)

*Dorset County Chronicle, Dorset – the County Magazine, The Salisbury and Winchester Journal, The Western Gazette, The Bournemouth Daily (*later *Evening) Echo, the Wimborne Journal.*

Index

*The names Wimborne, Wimborne Minster and minster church have not been included
as they occur so frequently in the text.*

Abbot Street, 40, 47
Ailrun, 16
Albion Inn, 72
Aldhelm, 12
Alfred, 10
Alim, Richard, 47
Alington, Lord, 87
Allen, River, 9, 11, 14, 15, 47, 50, 56, 57, 58, 60, 62, 68, 77, 81, 84
Allendale, 57, 58, 77, 84
almshouses, 33, 37, 49, 50, 51, 61, 62, 84
Angel Inn, 84
Anglo-Saxon Chronicle, 10, 12, 14
Anstey, John, 48
Aragon, Catherine of, 37
Ase, John, 42-3
Athelred, 10, 12
Avenue Road, 79, 80

Badbury Rings, 9, 12
Badeston, William de, 20
Baker, Thomas, 42
Bankes, Henry, 65
Bankes, Henry, Ralph, 87
Bankes, Sir John, 40
Bankes, John, 56, 65
Bankes, Lady Mary, 40
Bankes, Sir Ralph, 40, 41
Bankes, William John, 80
Barford, 15, 81
Barnes, John, 44, 59
Barnsley, 15, 38, 40, 47
Barratt, F.W. & Co., 87
Barry, Sir Charles, 80, 81
Bath, 60
Batt, William, 56
Beauchamp, Margaret, 36
Beaufort, John, 36
Beaufort, Margaret, 35, 36, 37, 38
Beck, W.J., 76
Bell Inn, 59
bells, 31, 36, 43, 51
Benedict, Pope, 22
Benton, Sir John, 34
Benyson, Simon, 37
Bercario, William, 29
Besant, Jane, 43
bishop, 12, 13, 18, 20, 35, 43, 83
Black Death, 27, 29, 32
Blake, Joseph, 58
Blandford, 24, 33, 60, 61, 62, 70, 78, 79, 87
blind house, 56, 83
Blount, James, 38, 49
Bodyn, John, 31
Boleyn, Anne, 37
Boniface, Pope, 22
Boniface, St., 13
borough, 18, 24, 25, 40
Bourne Valley, 77
Bournemouth, 66, 68, 76, 77, 79, 86, 87
Bower, Benjamin, 64
Bowle, Charles, 74
Boxley, Thomas, 49
Boyton, Captain, 81
Bradford, 15, 67, 81

Bradford Abbas, 47
Braffett, 63
Brembre, Thomas de, 23, 27, 37 42
Brewer, Mary, 46
bridges, 33, 57, 60, 62
Bridport, 17
Bristol, 20, 43, 56, 60, 83, 85
Brito, Ralph, 21, 22
Broadbent, John, 63
Broadstone, 78
Broomhill, 71
Brown, Alice, 50
Brown, Elizabeth, 58
Brownsea, 40
Bryan, Richard, 33
Buckyngham, Henry de, 23
Budden, Frank, 63
Buffett, Mary, 56
burgesses, 17, 18
Burghal Hidage, 12
Bushrod, Jesse, 81
Cambridge, 36, 50
Canford, 15, 18, 24, 38, 46, 49 62, 79, 81
canons, 20, 36, 37, 46
Canterbury, 46
Carlisle, 22
Case is Altered, The, 61
Castleman, 57, 58, 59, 68, 77, 78
Cemetary, 9, 80
Chained Library, 69, 70
chantries, 23, 33, 36, 37, 38, 42
Chapel Lane, 71
chapels, 19, 20, 21, 32, 33, 36, 37, 61, 69, 70
Charborough, 62, 79
Charles I, 38, 43, 52
Charles II, 52
charter, 38, 43
Chilbridge, 9, 23, 68
Chilmark, 47, 52, 80
Church Ale, 51
Church Cakes, 48
Church House, 84
church rate, 51
Church Street, 74
churchwardens, 27, 29, 31, 32, 34, 38, 51, 52, 53, 58, 62, 63, 64, 70
Christchurch, 35, 64
Civil War, 40, 52, 69
Clare, Richard de, 22
Clarke, Jane, 47
clock, 34, 65
cloth, 29, 31, 34, 36, 41, 47, 48, 52, 63
Clubmen, 52
Cluett, James, 59
Coach and Horses, 49, 60
cock-fighting, 48
Colbourne, Samuel, 55
Colchester, 22
Colehill, 14, 23, 29, 59, 70, 71, 79, 84, 85, 87
Coles Hardware, 73
College, 20, 27, 36, 37, 38
Collett's Charity, 50
commissioners, 37, 38, 49, 72
Commonwealth, 52

Community Centre, 58, 84
Conservative, 65, 75
Cook Row, 31, 47, 60
Corfe Castle, 40, 50, 65
Corfe Mullen, 24, 62, 75, 78
Corfton, de, 29
Cornish, Robert, 47
Cornische, John, 44
Cornmarket, 25, 30, 32, 47, 48, 63, 64, 65, 71, 84
Corporation, 38, 40, 43, 52, 67, 72, 83
Court House/Cottage, 27, 60
courts, 33, 43, 44, 46, 47, 55, 58, 59, 60
Cowdry, Henry, 83
Cowdry's Bakery, 72
Cowgrove, 14, 15, 27, 32, 40, 47, 50, 60, 62, 87
Cox, Peter, 48
Cox, Richard, 56
Cranborne, 60, 62, 74
Cribb, Robert, 83
Crichel, 17, 20, 87
Cromwell, 52
Crooked Withies, 41, 68
Cross, Sophia, 75
Crown and Anchor, 61, 62, 77
Crown Hotel/Inn, 21, 48, 78, 84
Cuthburga (Cuthburh), St., 10, 12, 13, 25, 32
Cwenburh, 10, 12, 13

Danish, 10, 14
dean, 14, 20, 21, 22, 24, 25, 27, 32, 36
Dean's Court, 40, 41, 49, 58, 65, 84, 87
Deck, 47
Delacourt, John, 42
Dewey's, 38
Dissenters, 46, 48
Dodo, 16, 19
Domesday, 9, 16, 17, 18, 19, 29
Dorchester, 9, 17, 55, 62, 78, 80
Downton, 24
Drax, J.S.W.S. Erle, 79
Due, Edward, 44
Duffall, William, 83
Duppleshegh, 23
Durman, Robert, 43
Dyson, John, 81
East Borough, 25, 26, 57, 62, 64 73, 83
East Brook Bridge, 44, 62
East Street, 77, 82
Easton, William, 48
Edward, 12
Edward the Confessor, 14, 17
Edward I, 21, 25
Edward III, 24, 32
Edward VI, 67
electricity, 77
Elizabeth I, 38, 43, 67
Elliott, Thomas, 44, 47
enclosure, 30, 66
Essex, 22
Ethelwold, 12
Eton, 36
Ettrick, Anthony, 56

Exeter, 16, 18, 49, 60
Eyers, William, 47

fair, 32, 35, 51
farming, 29, 58, 66, 78
Farr, John, 48
fire, 42, 62, 63, 64, 82, 83
Fisher, John, 35
Fitch, Henry, 56
Fitzgerold, Robert, 16, 19
Fitzparnell, William, 32
Fleming, Kaye le, 87
Fletcher, William, 73
Forist, Mary, 55
Forist, William, 47
Forward, George, 75
Fowler, Alexander, 46
Frampton, Anne, 43
Frampton, Thomas, 43
France, 41
Franconia, 13
Frenchmen, 19, 40
Frenschman, Gyllam, 40
Fryer, John, 56
Fryer, William, 64
Furzehill, 14

Galpin, James, 83
gas, 76, 82
Gaunt, John of, 32
George Inn, 25, 47, 48
George III, 64
Gerard, Thomas, 51
Germany, 13
Gertrude, Lady, 49, 84
Gilles, Comson, 44
Gillingham, Roger, 50, 51, 69, 77
Glamorgan, 56
Gloucester, 16
Glyn, John Carr, 75
Glyns, 65
God Blessing Green, 87
Godwin, 16, 19
Goldesney, Margaret, 47
Goldesney, William, 47
Govayr, John, 31
Grammar School, 11, 36, 38, 43, 49, 50, 65, 67, 69, 72, 73, 74
graveyard, 34
Green Man, 58
Greyhound, 48
Griffin Hotel, 85
Guest, F.E., 75
guild hall, 32
Gulliver, Isaac, 64
Gundry, Mary, 49
Gunpowder Plot, 44

Habgood, Richard, 50
Habgood, Robert, 44
Hall, Edith, 50
Hampreston, 20, 34, 35, 56
Handley Torches, 68
Hanham, Sir James, 59, 65
Hanham, John, 38, 40, 77, 78, 80
Hanham, Sir Michael, 40
Hanham, Richard, 40
Hanham, Thomas, 40, 80
Hanham, Sir William, 56, 65
Hannam (see Hanham)

Hardy, Thomas, 79
Hart, Thomas, 65
Hartlands, 65
Harvey, Ann, 55
Hastings, 17
Hawke, Peter, 74
Hearth Tax, 41, 89
Henry III, 20, 24, 32
Henry VI, 34
Henry VII, 35
Henry VIII, 35, 36, 37, 40
Henwood, Mr., 58
High Hall, 56, 65
High Street, 50, 65, 67, 73, 79
Hillbutts, 42, 61, 73
Hinton Martell, 17, 18
Hinton Moor, 66
Hiscock, Mary, 56
Hiscock, Robert, 56
Hodgekynnes, Richard, 36
Holland, William, 68
Holt, 15, 20, 32, 34, 40, 42, 44, 64, 66, 68, 70, 71, 84, 87
Holt Lodge, 41, 56
Home Guard, 85
Honeybrook, 62
Horne, William, 51
Horton, 18, 19
Hospital, 32, 33, 49, 77, 85

Ine, King, 12
Industrial Revolution, 76
Innocent, Pope, 33
inns, 32, 48, 62, 72

James I, 43
Jay, John, 47, 66
Jay, Thomas, 44
Jubber, William, 43
Julians Bridge, 62

King, Christopher, 56
King Down Farm, 67
King, John, 48
King's Arms, 48, 64
King Street, 55, 62, 65, 71, 74
Kingston Lacy, 9, 20, 24, 25, 26, 27, 29, 30, 32, 33, 34, 37, 38, 40, 41, 56, 61, 62, 63, 65, 66, 68, 70, 80, 81, 84, 87
Kingston Magna, 51
Knobcrook, 84

Lacey, Henry de, 35
Lacy, John de, 25, 27
Lake Gates, 9
Lambert, David, 56
Lanherne, 79
Lancaster, John Duke of, 32
Lancaster, Earls of, 27
Larmer Tree Grounds, 81
Lay Subsidy, 26, 27, 88
Leaze, The, 24, 26, 27, 32
Leicester, Earls of, 27, 32
Leigh, 14, 16, 19, 20, 24, 29, 34, 40, 47, 56, 62, 66, 70, 77, 84
Leland, John, 14, 27
Levelled Churchyard, The, 79
library, 43, 84
Lincoln, 22
Linen Hill, 14
Lioba, St., 13
Lisieux, 18
livestock, 18, 19, 24, 29, 35, 51, 58, 59, 66, 83
Llanderryn, 56
Lockey, Jordan, 25

Lodge Farm, 9, 26
London, 19, 38, 51, 60, 62, 70, 78
Long, George, 47
Longham, 62
Loope, Roger, 44, 47
Louch, Charles, 67
Lovell, Mr., 38
Lyne, Thomas, 50
Lytchett Matravers, 46

manor, 17, 18, 26, 27, 32, 34, 58, 60
manorial, 30, 55, 58, 59
Manston House, 80
market, 25, 30, 32, 35, 38, 43, 47, 51, 58, 78, 80
Martin, Leonard, 56
Masonic Hall, 71
Maud, Queen, 18
May, Elizabeth, 43
Melcombe Regis, 27
Mendip, 48
Middle Temple, 40, 50, 51
Miller, John, 44
Mitchell, Richard, 57
monastery, 12, 13, 14
Morris, Thomas, 44
Muster Rolls, 40

Nadder, River, 9
Napoleonic Wars, 69, 70
National Health Service, 77
National Trust, The, 80, 87
New Borough, 70, 80
New Forest, 60
New Inn, 48; 76
Newfoundland, 53, 55
Nicholas, Pope, 20
Norman, Thomas, 46
Normandy, 16, 18
Norhoor, William, 57
Northumbria, 12, 13
nunnery, 13

Oakley, Thomas, 56
Oddfellows, 80
Odeham (Odenham), 19
Official, 43, 65
overseers of the poor, 53, 55, 56, 58
Oxford, 36, 50

Pamphill, 15, 24, 26, 32, 50, 51, 60, 63, 65, 70, 77, 84, 87
Parker, Simon, 44
parliament, 37, 40, 52, 66
Parsons, John, 71
Patteshull, Martin de, 21, 25
Peculiar (see Royal Peculiar)
Penzance, 53
Percy, James, 55
Percy, Matthew, 55
Petersham, 19, 68
Phillips, Mrs., 57
Phyllypes, Master, 38
Piccadilly, 63
Piercy, Mary, 53
Pig Oak Farm, 68
Pillsmoor, 66
Pinson, Joan, 44
Pitney, William, 41
place-names, 14
plague, 27, 52
Plymouth, 71, 85
Pole, Reginald, 22
Poole, 33, 34, 38, 40, 42, 49, 52,

56, 60, 62, 64, 67, 68, 77, 78, 80, 81
Poor Law, 49, 53, 56, 57, 74, 89, 90
population, 27, 31, 53, 62, 70
Portland, 40
Portsmouth, 74
Post Office, 77
Povington, 19
Pratt, Sir Roger, 41
Priest's House Museum, 73, 83
Puddletown, 78
Purbeck, 19, 23, 47
Purchas, John, 44
Pye Corner, 62

Quarter Jack, 70

railway, 71, 76, 77, 78, 79, 80, 84
Raindle, John, 33
Raindle, Matthew, 57
Raven, Elizabeth, 56
Redcoddes, John, 33
Redcotts, 33, 43, 48, 58
Reformation, 13, 37, 40, 43, 44, 47, 51, 71
Restoration, 52, 53
Ringwood, 31, 50, 60, 62
roads, 23, 24, 33, 35, 58, 59, 60, 62
Roman, 9
Romsey, 48
Rotecod, John, 22
Rowden, Oliver, 59
Rowe, Thomas, 46
Rowlands, 9, 49, 70, 79
Royal Agricultural Society, 81
Royal Peculiar, 20, 21, 43, 46, 47, 52, 65, 83
Rushleys, 49
Russell, Nicholas, 56
Russell, Richard, 40

St. Anthony, 33, 37, 49
St. Catherine, 20, 34, 71, 80
St. James, 20, 32, 34, 35, 70
St. John, 70
St. Margaret, 32, 33, 37, 49, 61, 62, 80
St. Michael, 70
St. Paul's, 22
St. Peter, 20, 21, 34, 40, 52
St. Stephen, 20, 34, 35, 70
Salisbury, 20, 31, 51, 60
Salisbury, Earl of, 44
Salisbury, Edward of, 18
Sandell, Elizabeth, 46
Sandsfoot, 40
Saxons, 9, 14, 19
schools, 36, 38, 50, 51, 52, 55, 58, 69, 73, 74
Scott, George, 58
Selavestune, 19
Shaftesbury, 17, 34, 87
Shapwick, 17, 20, 23, 29
Sharpe, William, 33
Sherborne, 12, 20, 57, 67
Shittler, John, 81
Sigferth, 14
Siler, Christopher, 44
Simon the Labourer, 27
Skinner, Henry the, 31
Small, Henry, 81
Smith, Alice, 43, 44
Somerset, Duke of, 36
Southampton, 24, 31, 34, 62, 78, 85

spire, 38, 51, 52
Spruce, Grace, 44
Square, 20, 21, 29, 34, 40, 48, 52, 65, 75, 78
Stanbridge, 20
Stone, 40, 47, 62
Stone, Rev. William, 69
Stour, River, 9, 11, 15, 19, 33, 34, 47, 50, 60, 62, 80, 81
Strangeways, Sir Giles, 38
Street, Thomas, 58
Sturminster Marshall, 33
Sturts, 65
Sun Fire Insurance, 57, 63
Swan, Aldrich, 51
Sykes, James, 78

Tanner, John the, 31
taverns, 48, 64
Thornhill, 14, 40
Tilley, Mr., 86
tithes, 20, 38, 47, 67, 72
Tivoli Cinema, 65
Tory, Richard, 56
Tower, 34, 37, 63, 70, 71
Town Hall, 40
Town Mill, 60
Townley, Robert, 40
Trem (see Trime)
Trime, Margaret, 44, 46, 47
Tripet, John, 33
Tulloch, John, 70
turnpikes, 60, 61, 62, 78

Up Wimborne, 17
Urban District, 83

Vanna, Robert de, 22
Venice, 80
Victoria Hospital, 77
Victoria, Queen, 69, 74, 77
Vikings, 12, 14
Vindogladia, 9

Walford, 15, 18, 19, 23, 24, 47, 62, 84
Walker, Mrs., 63
Wallis, John, 51
Wareham, 9, 17, 63
water works, 76, 77
Webb, Sir John, 49
Wells, 20
Wessex, 10, 12, 14
West Borough, 24, 25, 26, 48, 62, 64, 65, 71, 72, 74
West Moors, 84
West Street, 62, 80
Weymouth, 27
White Hart, 25, 80
White, Mary, 55
White, Richard, 55
Whitelegge, 44
Whitemill Bridge, 33
Wilksworth, 18, 19
William the Conqueror, 9, 16
Wilton, 9
Win(n), River, 9, 14
Winchester, 24, 36
Woodmansheet, 34
workhouse, 56, 57, 65, 69, 74, 75
Wright, Richard, 56
Wylye, River, 9

Yates, Robert, 43
Yelde Hall, 32
Young, Henry, 44